Revisioning
Society & Culture

Selected and Introduced by Douglas Sloan
Series Editor: Robert McDermott

CLASSICS FROM THE

Journal for
ANTHROPOSOPHY

NUMBER 77   SPRING 2007

Cover image: *Lower String Sound*
By Martina Angela Müller
Front cover and layout: Seiko Semones
Series editor: Robert McDermott
Editor: Douglas Sloan

The Journal for Anthroposophy
1923 Geddes Ave., Ann Arbor, MI 48104
TEL 734.662.9355 FAX 734.662.1727

ISSN-0021-8235

Printed by McNaughton & Gunn, Inc., Saline, Michigan

CONTENTS

Classics from the *Journal for Anthroposophy*

Volume 1: *Meeting Rudolf Steiner*
Selected and Introduced by Joan Almon

Volume 2: *Anthroposophy & Imagination*
Selected and Introduced by Kate Farrell

Volume 3: *Revisioning Society & Culture*
Selected and Introduced by Douglas M. Sloan

Volume 4: *Meeting Anthroposophy*
Selected and Introduced by Robert Hill

Volume 5: *Science & Ecology*
Selected and Introduced by Arthur Zajonc

Series Editor: Robert McDermott

Introduction

Revisioning Society and Culture: The Transformation of Knowing

Douglas Sloan

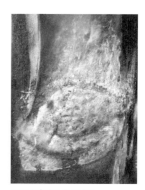

Lower String Sound by
Martina Angela Müller

This is the third special issue in the "Classics Series" of the *Journal for Anthroposophy*. The Classics Series has included articles selected from regular issues of the *Journal for Anthroposophy* published since 1965. The first issue in the "Classics Series" is devoted to articles dealing with Rudolf Steiner; the second focuses on imagination. The fourth issue will focus on the variety of ways to encounter Anthroposophy, and the fifth will reprint essays on science and ecology. This present issue presents perspectives on "Society and Culture."

As a heading for a small book, "Society and Culture" encompasses large, shifting categories. It is not surprising that sociologists, anthropologists, philosophers, and others, have conceived of society and culture in myriad and varying ways. If we consider "Society and Culture," however, at their most basic level, we do find a perspective not exhausted by such areas as "education," "science," "religion," and others. The concept of "culture" points to the nature of the consciousness that shapes a people's understanding of the world. In this sense, cultural consciousness would include basic assumptions about the nature of reality, and about how and what we can know of this reality, as well as a people's guiding values and attitudes toward life. The concept of "Society" points, then, to the actual social relations, institutions, and organizational structures that embody and give concrete expression to a people's cultural consciousness. The articles chosen for this issue of the *Journal for Anthroposophy* explore various anthroposophical perspectives on society and culture in this larger sense. They do not, either singly or together, present a systematic account of the relations between Anthroposophy and society and culture. They were not written for this purpose. Instead, each of the articles focuses on a specific social/cultural concern of our time and attempts to bring an anthroposophical perspective to bear on our understanding of it.

Throughout his life, Rudolf Steiner stressed repeatedly that the most crucial task facing the modern human being is that of transforming our dominant ways of knowing the world. This emphasis is the red thread that runs through and connects all Rudolf Steiner's writings, lectures, artistic work, and practical endeavors. Rudolf Steiner spoke of this transformation of knowing as developing the capacity to obtain genuine knowledge of the spirit. He spelled out in great detail what this entailed and its concrete implications for all of life. The articles in this issue of the *Journal* point, each in its own way and with respect to a particular social/cultural concern, to the necessity of this fundamental transformation of our knowing capacities.

KNOWLEDGE OF THE SPIRIT

Before introducing the specific articles contained in this issue of the *Journal*, it might be useful to consider briefly, and in the most general terms, this transformation of knowing such that it includes knowledge of the spirit. What would be its nature as knowledge of the spirit? Why is it necessary? What would be its consequences for society and culture? And, how are we, how can we be, and should we be, involved in this transformation?

Since the beginning of the scientific revolution in the seventeenth century in the West, three main assumptions about what we can know and how we know have dominated modern thinking and consciousness. These assumptions have had momentous consequences for all of modern life. The first assumption is what can be called the quantitative-mechanistic assumption about the ultimate nature of reality. It received its modern stamp very early in the scientific revolution in the distinction that was made at that time between what were designated as "primary qualities" and "secondary qualities." The primary qualities included such phenomena as extension in space, mass, weight, motion, number, and so forth. In other words, the realm of the primary qualities was essentially that of the quantitative. The primary qualities, it was thought, could be known with clarity and certainty through empirical description and mathematics. The secondary qualities at first included such phenomena as color, taste, and sound, but eventually were extended to include also other such qualitative domains as value, meaning, and purpose. In this view, knowledge as such was thought to apply only to the primary qualities, the quantitative. While the secondary qualities might well be realities of experience, they could not, strictly speaking, be known because they depended on the observer. In short, the perception of secondary qualities was considered to be tainted by subjective feelings, habits, predispositions, and so forth, and, consequently, could provide no proper material for precise, objective knowledge as such.

Accompanying this quantitative-mechanistic assumption were two further assumptions about what and how we can know. The first of these has been described as the "objectivistic assumption," which posits a fundamental separation between the knower and the object to be known. This assumption holds that if we want to know something properly, we must detach ourselves from it as completely as possible and describe it from the perspective of a mere, uninvolved onlooker. Appropriately, this assumption is also sometimes referred to as the assumption of the "onlooker consciousness." It was thought important not to intrude personal qualities involving feelings and values into the knowing relationship; to do so would distort and skew the pure knowledge of reality as objective and independent of the knower. The other assumption that accompanied this one has been called the "sensationist" or "sense-bound" assumption about knowable reality. This assumption, most forcefully expressed by the eighteenth century philosopher John Locke, holds that we can only know that which is given through our ordinary physical sense experience, and through abstractions from sense experience. This assumption about knowing further ensured the limitation of knowledge to the purely quantitative and mechanical.

At first the assumptions of this mechanistic view were applied mainly to nature. Nature, according to Descartes and Newton, was regarded as ultimately quantitative—without qualities and without consciousness.

It was to be understood entirely in terms of physical cause and effect, that is, mechanistically. Nature was regarded as essentially "a law-bound system of matter in motion." Gradually, during the nineteenth and twentieth centuries, this view was extended by many to the human realm and to the whole of society and culture. From this point of view, human beings themselves came also to be understood as essentially matter in motion. In this light, all human culture having to do with qualities and the non-material, such as meaning, values, purposes, ideals, and selves, came increasingly to be regarded as merely the surface manifestations—epiphenomena—of matter in motion.

The assumptions of the mechanical worldview have proved dramatically effective in dealing with the quantitative and mechanistic dimensions of the world. The power and achievements of modern technology in every area—in communication, travel, medicine, construction, computation, and so on—would have been impossible without the development over the past four centuries of ever-enhanced ways of knowing and dealing with the quantitative and mechanical dimensions of the world. Mechanistic assumptions are useful abstractions from the whole that are extremely effective precisely for understanding and working with the quantitative and the mechanical. When, however, these assumptions are extended to explain everything beyond the purely quantitative and mechanical, they become exceedingly destructive. Our experience of the life, the beauty, and the meaning in nature comes to be regarded as merely the complicated combinations of dead, passive, and valueless matter in motion. By definition—or really by fiat—the whole realm of the spirit is eliminated.

A fundamental transformation of our knowing would mean developing capacities for knowledge of the spirit, as well as of the material. In the most general sense, spirit refers to everything that is not matter, to all that is immaterial, to all that is non-sensory. What are these non-sensory realities, these realities of spirit? We have already mentioned them. They include meaning of every kind, including our ordinary ideas; values and ideals—the guiding ideas for achieving meaning; ultimate purposes and goals—formal and final ends; and qualities. Qualities include color, sound, and scent that are entwined with sense experience but whose full reality transcends the sensibly given—ask any artist if this isn't true. But qualities also include all that we experience as meaning, value, purpose, truth, beauty, goodness, freedom, love, and selves. Knowledge of the spirit can, therefore, also be described as knowledge of qualities in their fullest.

To develop capacities for non-sensory, qualitative knowledge—knowledge of spirit—would have far-reaching consequences for the whole of life, both individually and socially. The articles in this issue explore some of the important implications of such a transformation of knowledge. They also show that a transformation of our knowing capacities must perforce involve a fundamental transformation of ourselves: of our feelings, our conceptual abilities, our powers of attention and concentration, our attitudes, and values. Knowing in its fullness involves the whole human being. A transforming of our dominant modern ways of knowing such as to include knowledge of both the material and the spiritual, and their intimate interconnection, would also be a transformation of ourselves and of our world.

INTRODUCTORY REFLECTIONS ON
THE ARTICLES IN THIS ISSUE

The first article in this issue by Georg Kühlewind, "Michael—Spirit of the Times," addresses directly this most important task of the modern human being: the transformation of our knowing through meditative self-transformation. "Never," writes Kühlewind, "has such a stride been as urgent nor as possible as today." It is urgent because, as we shall consider later in more detail, the prevalent materialistic consciousness of our age becomes increasingly destructive. The transformation of this consciousness is possible as never before because, since the end of the nineteenth century, the "cosmic intelligence"—the non-sensory source of world creation—has been available to human beings in a new way. The guardian of the cosmic intelligence is the spiritual being known in western traditions as the Archangel Michael, who is also at various historical periods the spiritual leader of human culture. He makes it possible for human beings to begin the work of self-transformation, to connect once again with the living thoughts of world creation. In this view, human thinking itself can become newly enlivened and creative. In his many lectures on the Archangel Michael, Rudolf Steiner explained that Michael does not fit easily with conventional notions of spiritual beings in that he does not force his wisdom or his will upon human beings [or humanity]. Instead, in utter respect for human freedom, with only a beckoning gesture, he invites the human to begin the work of self-trans-formation as an act of freely chosen, self-responsibility. He does not ease the human being's way along this path of self-transformation. In fact, in one sense, embarking upon this path will increase obstacles and height-en life's difficulties, for it requires that one move against the currents of our familiar, conventional assumptions and social practices.

What Michael does offer is the gift and power of courage required to carry out the task of self-transformation. And because this task involves connecting anew with the living, qualitative thoughts of world creation, it has the broadest possible consequences for the transformation of sci-ence, of the arts, and of social life and institutions. To the extent that we continue to neglect Michael's invitation, the forces of cosmic intelli-gence are, as Kühlewind writes, "directed and distorted by the adversary forces and formed into ideas which are hostile and detrimental to humankind; this is what often happens." We see these distorted and detrimental ideas at the core of the dominant sense-bound and mecha-nistic assumptions of the modern mindset.

"Toward Meeting Evil with Consciousness," by Adeline Bianchi, adds to our understanding of why the transformation of consciousness is so cru-cial in our time. When and if we allow ourselves even a modicum of conscious awareness, the manifestations of evil today can be overwhelm-ing. And yet, Rudolf Steiner says that this awareness is necessary for in this and the following epoch of human evolution evil will become increasingly pervasive and powerful. It is the special task of human beings in our time to meet the growing presence of evil and begin the work of transforming it. Again, this requires self-transformation. There is no place in this approach for projecting all evil onto other people and other forces, the increasingly prevalent practice of nations at the present time. The practice of dissociating ourselves from the evil within and projecting it onto the other—"they are the axis of evil," "they are the great Satan"—is fallacious because the sources of evil lie within each of us. As Rudolf Steiner has written, "Since the beginning of the fifth post-Atlantean epoch [in the beginning of the fifteenth century] the propensity, the tendency for evil, lies in the subconscious of *every* person. . . . There is no crime, however dreadful, for which we as people of the fifth post-Atlantean epoch do not have the propensity." The transformation of evil requires self-transformation, which, in turn, needs Michaelic courage, for it must begin with an unflinching self-awareness.

One of the most important sources for the transformation of consciousness and of knowing is the entire field of art. Art—the aesthetic—is one of the human being's main connections with the whole realm of the qualitative. Qualities of life, newness, beauty, value, and so forth, are the substance of the artistic endeavor. The qualities contained in the artistic experience can nurture qualitative capacities and realities in us. At the same time, by our bringing qualities to birth within ourselves we can recognize and unite more fully with the qualities of the world. Art has the potential for deepening knowledge of qualities in all other areas of human life—science, religion, education, agriculture, economics, and others.

Yet, in our time, art seldom has this effect. Art itself has been seriously enfeebled by the modern limitation of knowledge to the purely quantitative, mechanical, and sense-bound. Art has too often been reduced to entertainment and mere embellishment. Moreover, the stance of the objectivistic onlooker consciousness, taken as the only proper attitude toward knowing, has helped push the artistic experience further into the realm of the merely subjective and irrational. In his brief and insightful discussion of the influential German artist, Joseph Beuys, "Joseph Beuys-The Protest Against Materialism's Deformed Image of Man," Diether Rudloff shows how art is diminished by the assumption that we can have knowledge only of the quantitative and mechanistic. This, as he puts it, has had the effect of "reducing science to a one-dimensional rationalism" and "the breaking off of all connection with humanity, nature, and the cosmos, as well as cutting off art from the wellsprings of life."

It was just this realization that Joseph Beuys expressed through his art. Drawing upon the harrowing experiences of World War II, illuminated by his own deep study of Rudolf Steiner, he set himself the task of exploring how art could once more become a prime force in the "development of human consciousness." Because this meant for Beuys breaking most of the conventional canons of what constitutes art, he remains today, a generation after his death in 1986, one of the most discussed and controversial of modern artists.

Another example of the critical importance of art, not as mere embellishment but as a carrier of qualities that can nurture and give expression to the wholeness of the human being, is provided by Rex Raab's article, "The Survival of Architecture." The center of Raab's article is Rudolf Steiner's two Goetheanum buildings in Dornach, Switzerland, as the central research center for the work of Anthroposophy in the world. After the first Goetheanum, to which Rudolf Steiner devoted ten years of unstinting dedication, was destroyed by an arsonist on New Year's Eve, 1922, Rudolf Steiner set about immediately to draw up plans for its replacement, the second Goetheanum, which was completed only after Steiner's death.

Raab describes the two Goetheanums and the pioneering directions opened by each for the future of a new architecture. After the destruction of the first Goetheanum, which was constructed of wood, Steiner immediately moved to design a building to be made of poured, reinforced concrete, one of the first of its kind and still studied by architects from around the world. As Raab's account brings out, both buildings were designed to stand as organic unities, each part expressing the whole, and the whole giving the impression of constant movement and integral connection among the parts. Each incorporated all of the arts—sculpture, painting, and facilities for speech, movement, and drama. Each of the buildings represented an attempt to provide an architectural environment hospitable to and supportive of the human being.

Something of the larger cultural significance of the new artistic impulses represented in the two Goetheanums, can perhaps be grasped by looking at the term "postmodernism." Although it remains extremely vague and amorphous, "postmodernism" in general refers to movements that acknowledge the passing of modern social/cultural forms, and the creation of "postmodern," less definable, or deliberately non-definable, forms more adequate to the sweeping changes that the "modern" world has undergone. "Postmodernism" is often used to cover a range of changes in nearly every aspect of modern life that have been described variously as "post-colonial," "post-industrial," "post-national," "post-structural" (in philosophy), "post-religion," "post-Enlightenment," "post-patriarchal," "post-ideological," and so on.

Much of the postmodern movement has been largely a critical movement, often described under the heading of "deconstructive postmodernism," a movement devoted to critiquing and deconstructing the dominant assumptions of modern thought and culture. This movement has had many beneficial results in that it has revealed some of problems and illusions as well as the oppressive nature of "modernist" assumptions and practices. But it has been much less effective in providing positive directions for the future. To use a term originated by the process philosopher David Ray Griffin, what is urgently needed now is what he calls a "constructive postmodernism."[1]

With respect to this article, it may be especially significant that the term "postmodernism" first arose in the field of architecture. In architecture the term "modern," other than a general expression simply for what is up-to-date and contemporary, came to be attached to particular styles, most notably the Bauhaus style—the sparse, utilitarian structure now often represented in the modern, urban office building. Architects who have wanted to break with the modern have often drawn upon a reservoir of different styles from the far past and modern present, and put them together in almost collage-like designs as postmodern. These often have a certain novelty, and sometimes do suggest points of genuine constructive departure for the future. But even this movement, while it tries to go beyond modernism, which it critiques, has yet to develop fully into a genuinely positive, constructive postmodernism. By contrast, in his designs for the two Goetheanum buildings Steiner not only moved beyond the modern, but also provided indications as to what a truly constructive postmodernism in architecture could be.

The topic of postmodernism would seem to suggest a new way of understanding Anthroposophy itself. Is it possible that in all he said and did, Rudolf Steiner had in mind not so much his contemporaries, but more so those of future generations? Perhaps the awareness of what the future demands, which Steiner once attributed to Goethe, applies just as strongly to Steiner himself. "Goethe," he said, "was not only a man of his time; he was inwardly able to look ahead to the twentieth century and wrote Part Two of Faust for the twentieth, twenty-first and later centuries."[2] Steiner might also have been addressing primarily those of future generations who would experience and recognize the challenge of trying to live creatively in a postmodern world. In this light, we today, and those who will follow us, perhaps have a better opportunity, are better situated, to understand Rudolf Steiner and Anthroposophy than many of his own time. If Steiner was one of the first constructive postmodernists, then it would seem to be our challenge to try to understand his worldview and the practices he recommended within a constructively postmodern context—to move beyond and seek to transform the fixed, materialistic structures of modern consciousness, to begin to engage Anthroposophy, and from it the world, with the openness, the qualitative awareness, and the readiness to live in uncertainty that our postmodern situation demands.

In his article, "The Spiritual Heart of Service: Self-Development and the Thinking Heart," Cornelius Pietzner describes service to others as itself a path of spiritual development. He distinguishes service from charity. Charity as commonly conceived and practiced, he writes, is a one-way transaction, from the giver to the receiver. In service, the relationship between server and served is two-directional, as a result of which both server and served are fundamentally changed in the process. In order truly to serve, we must have the capacity to receive and to learn from the other. Service itself becomes a path of self-transformation.

Pietzner focuses especially upon the need to develop our feelings. Rather than being satisfied with our ordinary feelings of self-centered likes and dislikes we can strengthen and purify our feelings to make them true organs of cognition. "Thinking with the heart," as he puts it, is the experience of a feeling life capable of opening receptively and sensitively to a world beyond our ordinary self-absorption. It is through the "thinking heart," through cognitive feelings, that we come to know most immediately the qualities of spirit. Service itself, as Pietzner shows, is a work of self-transformation on the path of knowledge of the spirit.

Both spirit itself and knowledge of the spiritual realities it engenders are desperately needed in our world.

In "Working Together as an Aspect of Inner Development," Christopher Schaefer also explores the urgent task of self-transformation. He begins by noting Rudolf Steiner's observation that, in the future, antisocial forces stemming from a heightened sense of individuality will become ever stronger. Special efforts must therefore be made to develop social forces to counter and balance the anti-social. This, says Schaefer, requires two developments: first is the creation of new social forms and structures to foster and support the necessary new social relationships of equality and interdependence among human beings. Underlying this, and making it possible, is the second requirement, the development within ourselves of inner capacities for social life. Again, self-transformation is shown to be essential to social and moral development.

Schaefer describes the strong tendencies within each of us that stand in the way of developing social, as opposed to anti-social, forces. These obstacles manifest as our "double" in the forms of doubt, unrefined sympathies and antipathies, and egotism. These, he shows, must be countered within ourselves by interest, understanding, and compassion. The cultivation of the social capacities can only take place through the full development of our soul faculties—thinking, feeling, and willing, all working together to recognize and accept the spiritual reality of the other. At a time of mounting worldwide conflict, it becomes increasingly evident, as Schaefer concludes, that the future of human society and of the earth is at stake.

The possibility of a form of social organization that can support the fullness of human life in every dimension—political, economic, and cultural—is the subject of Clopper Almon's article, "Ideas that Destroyed Russia and Ideas that Can Rebuild." At first glance, this article might seem to be dated. It was written with reference to a specific world event—the collapse of the Soviet Union at the end of the 1980s. Since then, the hopes for the kind of meaningful social-economic reform in Russia that Almon saw as a real possibility have not been fulfilled. Moreover, many other important events of a social/economic nature have taken place since then—among them, for example, the event of

September 11, 2001, the two Iraqi wars, the rise and bursting of the technology investment bubble, the fall of Enron, and so forth. Yet, a closer reading of the article will reveal that these later events convincingly exemplify the crucial importance of Almon's case for "Ideas that Can Rebuild"—ideas that western society, as well as the rest of the world, have yet to understand and put into practice.

In presenting the essence of these ideals, Clopper Almon gives an exceedingly clear and succinct explication of what in Anthroposophy is known as Rudolf Steiner's conception of the "Threefold Social Order." It is refreshing, however, that Almon never explicitly refers to this phrase. If simply mouthed without understanding, the expression easily becomes a mere slogan, either a kind of talisman, which, as if repeated enough, would magically usher in basic social change, or a form of shibboleth used dogmatically to distinguish the "genuinely serious" anthroposophist from the not-so-serious.

Avoiding this possible sloganizing of the term, Clopper Almon concentrates on understanding what is actually involved. He looks carefully at the three major functions of human life—the political, the economic, and the cultural—as these arise in response to basic human needs. He shows how each of these functions ideally has its own distinctive identity and integrity and, at the same time, stands in an interpenetrating relation with the others. He points to the distortions in social life that occur when one or another of the functions—such as the economic, particularly in the United States—is allowed to overwhelm and dominate the others. He also indicates how an understanding and realization of the proper relations among these three functions can address the modern problems of narrow forms of nationalism as well as an overweening global economism. He shows that all three—the political, the economic, and the cultural—are impoverished by the modern materialistic assumptions that separate each of them from their true spiritual depths and, consequently, are even made to subvert the real human needs they are meant to serve. A healthy, full-bodied cultural life is essential as the source of freedom, newness, and creativity in the other realms, which in turn can then help make possible a fully functioning cultural life.

In his brief and profound article, "From Consumer to Producer in the

Spiritual Sphere," Herbert Witzenmann reflects on our deeply entrenched, modern consumer consciousness, and on the desire, nevertheless, of many people—young people especially—to break free of the consumer mentality and instead to become productive contributors to society. As Schaefer and Almon also argue, the transformation of the consumer culture requires new social forms, but, as they also emphasize, it requires an inner transformation, the development of new capacities for knowing and acting in the world.

The violence, lovelessness, and pitilessness, rampant in our world go unchecked by the consumerism at the heart of modern economism. Indeed, the progressive brutalization of the world feeds on the apathy and selfishness of a society of consumers, obsessed with self-seeking and the insatiable accumulation of material goods and pleasures. This consumerism is made possible, furthermore, by the forced labor of the world's poor and unprotected, so that the consumer mentality stands as a constant obstacle to concerns for justice and the exercise of mercy. It also encourages the unrestrained exploitation of the earth at the expense of all future generations, human and others. At the same time, the intensity of the consumer mentality is constantly stoked by the fear that there will not be enough to go around. The readiness to suppress all natural feelings of empathy and mercy toward others and to resort to violence against the other is further fed by such fear. The popular materialism of unrefined and unrestrained desire at the heart of the consumer culture finds added support in the much deeper materialism of modern consciousness which sees the world ultimately as nothing but matter in motion, void of meaning, love, and life, and, therefore, susceptible to being plundered at will.

To move beyond a narrow consumer society means overcoming the consumer impulse in oneself. Witzenmann provides a concrete example of the self-observation and meditative work this task of inner development requires. In this inner transformation new, independent, and powerful will forces are generated. Feelings become oriented to receive rather than only to take. Thinking, fed by new willing and feeling forces, acquires the capacity to experience as knowable realities the myriad qualities of meaning, love, and life. In the place of a constantly taking, and ultimately death-dealing, consumerism, the productiveness of a life-affirming, life-generating presence in the world can arise.

In "The Bio-Dynamic Movement in Our Time," the late Herbert Koepf introduces one of the most important social and cultural impulses initiated by Rudolf Steiner. It is sometimes overlooked that agriculture is ultimately the foundation of all society and culture. Our relationship to the land, the plants, and the animals, and our care of them—or lack thereof—directly affects the quality of our human life together. That the cosmos, human community, and the earth are intimately interrelated is reflected directly in the words 'cultus,' 'culture,' and 'agriculture.' The nurture and tending of one redounds to the life and health of the others, just as the neglect and abuse of one becomes in the end disastrous for all.

Rudolf Steiner recognized early in the twentieth century that the human future will turn in a major way on a knowledge and practice of an agriculture that renews, rather than depletes, the earth, that fosters a vital plant life, that values the animals and cares for them, and that provides human beings with food that is nourishing. These have been the aims of biodynamic agriculture from its beginning.

In 1924 Rudolf Steiner delivered the first lectures on the principles of biodynamic agriculture to a group of farmers and gardeners. Koepf published his essay in the *Journal for Anthroposophy* in 1966, forty-two years after Rudolf Steiner's lectures; it is republished here forty-two years after its first publication. In this article, Herbert Koepf provides an introduction to Biodynamics, and also identifies many developments of modern agriculture that he astutely recognized would continue to grow in influence. Koepf rightly saw that an industrial, mechanized theory and practice of agriculture would continue to spread and to assert its dominance on a global scale. He also saw that in a growing recognition of the inadequacies and dangers, scientific and social, of industrialized agriculture, more and more efforts would appear, as they have in recent decades, to promote alternative forms of "organic agriculture," of which biodynamic agriculture is certainly one of the most important.

The industrial model of agriculture has been able to commend itself for several reasons. Through massive application of chemical fertilizers and pesticides, and by increasingly widespread implementation of irrigation, it has been possible to increase crop yields dramatically. This has gone hand in hand with the industrialization of animal husbandry—factory farming—as millions of animals are herded together in high density confinement, in barns and feedlots, completely removed from contact with the earth, and turned into packaged meat products by an assembly-line, slaughterhouse efficiency as soon as they can be fed and fattened. And by means of modern distribution systems it has been possible to supply the modern megalopolis with food supplies of staggering variety grown thousands of miles from their final destination.

But this has all taken place at a tremendous price, a price that is becoming increasingly unsustainable. The intensive application of chemical (petroleum-based) fertilizers and powerful pesticides produces, at first, high yields. The nutrient quality of the foods grown, however, diminishes steadily, even as their size and appearance are made ever more standardized and cosmetically appealing. The runoff and seepage from massive fertilizer and pesticide application are a major source of pollution of rivers, oceans, and underground water supplies. Intensive irrigation depletes precious underground aquifers. In many parts of the world, including North America, pollution and the drying up of rivers and aquifers now threaten both future drinking water supplies and large scale crop production dependent on irrigation. Pesticides adhere to almost all fruits and vegetables, and pesticide-resistant hybrid weeds and insects are increasingly in evidence. To prevent rampant spread of disease among animals confined in high density conditions, massive doses of antibiotics must be administered to them. Antibiotics then make their way directly into human tissues, and linger as well in the environment. Meanwhile, it goes almost unnoticed that the animals in this system—poultry, hogs, and cows—endure lives of unrelieved suffering.

Socially and culturally, the industrial, mechanistic model of agriculture has been similarly destructive. For the system to work, land must be appropriated and consolidated in the hands of a relative few, either a few large landowners, or, increasingly, large corporations whose headquarters are usually far distant from the land itself. During the twentieth century, millions of small farmers have accordingly been forced off the land by relentless government and corporate policies aimed at gaining control and profits made possible by the practice of industrial agriculture. As a result, whole communities, once vital and thriving, have withered and died, economically and culturally. As corporations and government trade policies work together to impose industrialized agriculture globally, millions of farmers throughout the world are being forced from their lands and into rapidly expanding urban slums. The development of genetic engineering and patent rights on living organisms gives further control over agricultural profits to a few corporations as farmers world-over are now threatened with the loss even of their millennia-long right to save and plant what were once their own seeds. Cultural and environmental destruction have proven to be mutually reinforcing.

The rise of organic agriculture represents a crucial effort to reclaim the earth and its fruits for its own sake and for the benefit of all beings, animal and human that depend upon it. While biodynamic agriculture participates in the larger, general organic movement, it also contributes its own unique—and what its practitioners consider essential—insights and practices to the wider movement. Biodynamic agriculture shares in the multifold promise of all organic agriculture: among others, the production of foods of superior taste and nutritional value; foods free from pesticides, antibiotics, and disease; conservation of the soil and water supplies; almost no pollution; an intimate and mutually beneficial reciprocity between farmer and local community; and a respect for, and humane treatment of, the animals.

More specifically, biodynamic agriculture adds at least four unique contributions to the general organic movement. One contribution is a detailed understanding of the life forces of the earth with the development of practical methods for fostering and strengthening the life forces, life processes, and life substances essential for the future sustainability of all agriculture. A second contribution is a deep understanding of the integral relationships among Earth, plants, animals, and human beings. A third is the recognition of the need, as Herbert Koepf noted forty-two years ago, "to find new approaches to organizing the relation between producers and consumers in a way that benefits both." The rise and spread, since his article, of community supported agriculture (CSA) has represented an important, major step in meeting this need. In recent years CSA farms have continued to multiply throughout the country, serving big cities as well as towns and villages. As Herbert Koepf intimated, however, this can be only a first step in developing a full-fledged relationship between producers and consumers, the need for which biodynamic farmers are especially aware and for which they find many new possibilities in Rudolf Steiner's conception of the Threefold Social Order. A fourth, and centrally important contribution of Biodynamics is its unique understanding and detailed methods of cultivating the integral relationship between plants and animals and their earthly and cosmic environments.

As Herbert Koepf also stresses, the possibility of a new agriculture ultimately rests on an awakened and widespread consciousness of its need and on a resolute commitment to its realization.

In "Choosing America as a Place for Incarnation or Immigration in the 20th Century," Virginia Sease explores the question, "Which spiritual beings are especially active in America, and what is their nature?" As we have noted in these introductory reflections, Rudolf Steiner stressed the crucial importance for modern people to transform their knowing capacities in order to be able to take up such questions. In countless lectures, Steiner presented the results of his own spiritual scientific research. He did not ask that people accept his findings as a matter of faith, but that they at least seek to understand what he presented, to understand it as part of their own work in transforming their own knowing capacities. Steiner presented many descriptions of the qualities of the world hidden to ordinary consciousness, qualities that he said were manifestations of multitudes of beings—non-sensory centers of agency—some creative, some destructive in their working. He gave names to these beings, names that he often drew from various traditions which had recognized some of the essential qualities of these beings. He often pointed to other qualities of the beings in question which had, hitherto, remained hidden or had only emerged subsequently in the course of earth evolution. Repeatedly, he stressed that the names as such are not important, but that it is important to seek to discern, beginning with our ordinary consciousness and common sense, the quality and the nature of the work of these beings in the world.

Virginia Sease identifies some of the main beings from Rudolf Steiner's findings and the particular qualities of their relationships to America. The reader will note that Virginia Sease does not simply assert the existence of these beings, but seeks to identify the nature and quality of their presence and functioning in the world, as their activity can be perceived and experienced, to start with, by our ordinary consciousness. We must "learn," as she puts it, "to read the signature," the outer manifestation of these beings in their effects on the world and in human affairs.

Among the beings whose work she describes are the various doubles, which have a particular relationship to the geography of North America and often work destructively. Countering them are high beings of wisdom—the Kyriotetes as they are called in esoteric Christianity. Together with the Christ—the ground of the human eternal I—the Kyriotetes make it possible to transform the double, through free, life-giving ideas and ideals. She points to those dimensions of the human soul most vulnerable to the doubles, and to those dimensions in which the counterforces of life and love can be nurtured and activated.

Everything depends, however, on the development of qualitative-spiritual-capacities of knowing. In the words of Rudolf Steiner, which Sease, quotes: "To find living ideas, living concepts, living viewpoints, living feelings, not dead theories, that is the task of this age." And that also may be one way of describing the crucial task of the cultural sphere in Steiner's conception of the Threefold Social Order. It is the primary function of the cultural sphere to provide the living knowledge of meaning, value, purpose, and qualities that can guide and set a context for the humane functioning of the political and economic spheres. The Threefold Social Order in this sense is especially relevant to America's influence, for both good and ill, in today's world, and has special relevance to this article on America. As Steiner warned after World War I: "The Anglo-American world may gain world dominion; but without the Threefold Social Order it will, through this dominion, pour out cultural death and cultural illness over the whole earth."[3] For those today who are convinced, and have weighty reasons for so thinking, that the doubles have come overwhelmingly to the fore in present day America, Virginia Sease also reminds us of the particular spiritual realities with which we may still work in the hope that, in Abraham Lincoln's words, "the better angels of our nature" may yet prevail.

SOCIETY, CULTURE, AND
THE TRANSFORMATION OF KNOWING

In this concluding part of this introduction, we will explore the point emphasized by all the articles in this issue of the *Journal for Anthroposophy*, namely, the necessity for a fundamental transformation in our dominant ways of knowing. This part of the introduction is not presented as the anthroposophical view of the matter at hand. As Rudolf Steiner stressed again and again, there is no such thing as the anthroposophical view. As he stated late in his life: "In our time each person who is a member of a society like this one has to be a really free human being. Views, thoughts, opinions are held only by individuals. The Society does not have an opinion. And that should be expressed in the way that individuals speak about the Society. The *we* should actually disappear."[4] Of course, every effort is here made by the writer to reflect as responsibly as possible as an anthroposophist on our present social/cultural situation. This is done with the caution to the reader that the writer's understanding both of Anthroposophy and of the social/cultural situation may be flawed. With that due caveat in mind we still must not shrink from the task of trying to understand and respond as anthroposophists to present conditions and events, and all that they seem to portend.

We began by considering three central assumptions of modern consciousness, the first being the quantitative, mechanistic nature of all reality; the second is the sense-bound nature of all that we can know, namely, that we can only know that which is given through physical sense perception or abstractions from sense perception; the third is the objectivistic assumption that in knowing we must stand back as onlookers completely detached from the object of our observation and knowledge. It is important to bear in mind that these assumptions have become deeply ingrained in modern consciousness. To the extent that we embody modern consciousness, we all share in these assumptions to a greater or lesser degree. It is important to be aware that they often reassert themselves in our thinking even when we least expect it, even when we are engaged in trying to overcome them.

In what follows, we will ask, first, what have been the main criticisms historically of these assumptions of modern consciousness; second, in light of these criticisms, do these assumptions still hold, and to what effect; and third, what have been the main consequences of these assumptions for the human being and for the world.

1. Criticisms of the Mechanistic Assumptions

Before looking at the criticisms as such, it may be worthwhile, first, to consider briefly the main attempt to accept and come to terms with the mechanical worldview, an attempt which has sought, at the same time, to maintain a firm place for human values. This response can be described as the "two-realm theory of truth." It is most clearly represented in the long familiar distinction made between the truths of natural science and the truths of the humanities. This twofold approach to truth has a long history in western civilization. It was given its peculiarly modern cast very early in the scientific revolution by the distinction that, as we have seen, was made between the primary and the secondary qualities. During the eighteenth and nineteenth centuries, this two-realm theory of truth was further refined. It became institutionalized in the modern university, and remains so today, where it exerts its influence throughout the whole of modern education and culture. Science deals with nature, which, of course, is taken to include the human body. The humanities, as the name suggests, have as their purview, the strictly human realm of meaning, values, purpose, and qualities. In this division, only the "truths of science," dealing, through empirical observation and mathematics, with nature conceived as matter in motion, are viewed as objective knowledge. The "truths of the humanities," dealing as they do with the realm of secondary qualities, are limited to the subjective realms of faith, tradition, feeling (aesthetic, religious, and cultural), social custom, social action, and so forth.

This division between science and the humanities (in the German university: the *Naturwissenschaften*—the natural sciences and the *Geisteswissenschaften*—in English the humanities; in German, literally the spiritual sciences) has had a tremendous influence in shaping the society and culture of the West. In the face of a thoroughgoing mechanistic science, this affirmation of the humanities alongside the natural sciences has helped keep alive essential human qualities and concerns. Though merely subjective, and in that respect generally regarded by the dominant paradigm as inferior to scientific knowledge, the humanities have been a major source for the creative pursuit of human meaning and values. At their best, the humanities have helped cultivate a humanely critical spirit that has often stood as a bulwark against doctrinaire, and even political, infringements upon human freedom and human rights. The affirmation of the two-realm theory of truth has been the main response of modern religious thinkers who have been eager to reconcile their faith commitments with the materialism of modern science. It seems also to have been the main response of those scientists who are serious about both their scientific profession and their personal faith and ethical concerns. It would be difficult to overestimate the influence for good this two-realm theory of truth has had for modern, western society and culture. Nevertheless, the theory has some extremely serious problems, including several that have become increasingly acute.

A major problem, often not recognized, is that the science/humanities division expresses, and institutionalizes, from the start, a deep alienation of the human being from nature. Nature, handed over to science, is seen as dead matter in motion. Completely separated from this nature, and standing over against it, are the humanities—the strictly human concerns of meaning, purpose, value, and qualities. This division at the heart of our education system has helped produce a profoundly split consciousness in western civilization.

A second problem is that, while in theory the relationship between the two sides is supposed to be symmetrical and balanced, in practice it turns out to be quite unequal. In this division, as in racial segregation, separate has not been equal. The quantitative side is nearly always regarded as the more important. This becomes especially clear in education, for instance, when in times of financial exigency the first subjects to be eliminated in budget cutting are the arts and literature, not chemistry, physics, or computer science. In the university, the subjects dealing with the qualitative—literature, philosophy, education, religion, the arts—are constantly on the defensive, often tempted to show themselves more quantifiable and empiricist to prove that they stand on an equal footing in the curriculum with the natural sciences.

Finally, the most serious problem is the tendency for the mechanistic side to constantly encroach upon the humanities, such that all semblance of a symmetrical, equal relationship disappears. The claim is increasingly made that human beings and all that makes them uniquely human—meaning, values, ideals, love, their selfhood—can be understood like everything else in terms of matter in motion. The mechanistic view not only attempts to explain nature, but also to explain away the human. This tendency has become especially strong in contemporary western culture, with profoundly negative consequences, as explored below.

A growing recognition that the science/humanities two-truth dichotomy has serious problems, at least the three just mentioned, has led to challenges to the mechanistic worldview. Each of the three central assumptions of modern consciousness that we have looked at has been subjected, especially during the past century, to a number of penetrating critiques. We must ask to what extent, if any, these criticisms have dislodged the dominance of the mechanistic view and its claim to be the only source of genuine knowledge.

The assumption of the objectivistic, onlooker view of knowing has been, perhaps, the most thoroughly criticized of the three. The most important criticism has come from quantum physics, a central principle of which states that in the process of knowing the observer actively participates in and actually alters the state of what is being observed. This almost total abandonment of the old, detached onlooker stance in knowing by modern physics is especially telling since it was within physics that the ideal of the detached onlooker was originally, and quite dogmatically, advanced. The assumption of the detached onlooker has also been challenged by participatory conceptions of knowing coming from several other directions. Ecological studies and women's studies, for example, both stress that the deepest knowledge, whether of nature or of human beings, requires an interactive, participatory relationship between the knower and the known.

The mechanistic assumption itself has been challenged, again, by modern physics. The renowned theoretical physicist, David Bohm, is often quoted as having said, "It is now clear that no mechanical explanation [of the physical universe] is now available." Process philosophers have also challenged the mechanistic view by arguing that the most adequate metaphor for understanding nature is not the machine, but the living organism.

Finally, the assumption that all genuine knowledge is sense-bound has been called into question from several sides. Perhaps the most important challenge to the sense-bound (or sensationist) assumption has come from philosophers who point out that we must presuppose a certain intuitive apprehension of non-sensory realities even for the possibility of ordinary sense-bound knowing. The Whiteheadean philosopher and theologian David Ray Griffin has argued, for example, that the assumption that we can have no intuition and perception of nonsensory realities (such as ideas, moral norms, meaning, cognitive rules of logic) "makes impossible any empirical grounding for many ideas that are inevitably presupposed in all our practice, including our practice of science."[5] Every creative insight, whether in science or in other areas, involves, in the act of knowing, a grasp of new, nonsensory, qualitative realities. From this perspective, a major task confronting us today is to strengthen and further develop our capacities for new insight such that we can come to know the realm of qualities with the rigor, constancy, and penetration necessary for the full transformation of knowing that our times require.

2. Persistence of the Mechanistic Assumptions

These challenges to the assumptions of the modern mindset are important. They point to new possibilities. Anthroposophists need to be aware of such criticisms and be willing to cooperate with those, mostly non-anthroposophists, who are in the forefront of developing them. At the same time, however, we must ask, "How effective have the criticisms been up to this point? What is needed to bring the positive potential for knowledge of the spiritual, the qualitative, to full fruition?" In spite of the criticisms leveled at the mechanical philosophy from a number of quarters, it remains the dominant view not only of modern science but also of practitioners of other disciplines who have not established an objective, or spiritual-empirical, epistemology for their disciplines. In spite of the fact, for example, that modern physics, as we have seen, contains certain fundamental challenges to non-partici- patory ways of knowing and to an exclusively mechanistic interpretation of reality, modern physics still remains purely quantitative. The quanti- ties involved are essentially number, force, and motion, and, though these are dealt with in highly rarified, formal ways, they are, nevertheless, thoroughly quantitative. The physicists themselves are under no illusions that theirs is other than a quantitative enterprise, and as a matter of course they still often describe their field not as quantum physics, but as quantum mechanics. Moreover, most physicists have limited themselves to a purely instrumentalist approach that does not even ask about the larger implications of their subject. Instead, they still see it as their task to develop mathematical formulae that enable them to predict the outcome of further experiments and observations. These aspects of modern physics have yet to be taken into account by those who are quick to draw conclusions about a presumptive new spirituali- ty contained in quantum physics.

Another major field of scientific research today, that of cognitive science (brain research), is exceedingly mechanistic and reductionistic. Mind is identified entirely with brain, and the whole of the human being is reduced to the functioning of the neurons in the brain and nervous system. All of this is interpreted strictly mechanistically. The late Francis Crick, the biologist who turned to cognitive science after his work on DNA, has described the fundamental view of modern cognitive science this way:

> You, your joys and sorrows, your memories and your ambitions, your sense of personal identity, are in fact no more than the behaviour of a vast assembly of nerve cells and their associated molecules— you're nothing but a pack of neurons.[6]

Lest one suppose that this is the view of only one individual, consider this statement in which Crick was joined by the biologists Richard Dawkins and E.O. Wilson and the humanists Isaiah Berlin, W.V. Quine, and Kurt Vonnegut. In this statement, which they issued as a justification for unfettered scientific leeway to proceed with the cloning of higher mammals and human beings, they say:

> Humanity's rich repertoire of thoughts, feelings, aspirations, and hopes seems to arise from electrochemical brain processes, not from an immaterial soul that operates in ways no instrument can discover.[7]

The mechanistic reduction of the human being here is complete (and, of course, it goes completely unchallenged by the simplistic conception of soul that is proposed as an alternative). When scientists write in this way, it would seem necessary to conclude that they are making exceptions for themselves. If not, why would they expect us to pay any more attention to their electrochemical brain processes rather than our own? The fact that this apparently has not occurred to them, or that it has not led them to modify their worldview, indicates how deeply ingrained the mechanistic view is in the modern scientific mind.

Finally, in Neo-Darwinism, the dominant contemporary theory of evolution, the mechanistic assumptions reign supreme. In fact, neo-Darwinism as the sole and exclusive explanation of all evolution means the extension of the materialistic, mechanistic assumptions to the whole of life. The fundamental principle of neo-Darwinian theory holds that all of life must be regarded as a law-bound system of matter in motion (in which the "laws of chance" are central). In the past decade neo-Darwinism has received new impetus and standing within the university as the ideological rationale for unrestrained genetic engineering. As the distinguished geneticist and biochemist Mae Wan Ho has pointed out in her critique of genetic engineering, neo-Darwinism (as its champions themselves never tire of intoning) regards the whole of creation as a random product, a vast accident. It is what it is by chance; it could just as easily have been something else.

Since all is random, no reason exists why genes cannot be transferred from species to species—indeed, from kingdom to kingdom—at will, with patents taken out on the results, payable to the universities and their associated pharmaceutical and agribusiness partners. Materialist assumptions about knowable reality, financial profit, institutional structures,

greed, and a furious assault on nature all coalesce as a unity. One of the
tragedies of the current battle between neo-Darwinists and biblical cre-
ationists (both fundamentalist in their own ways) is that the reputable
biologists who accept evolution, but not an exclusively Darwinian interpretation of it, are attacked by both sides and eliminated from the discussion.

Despite cogent criticisms brought against it, the mechanistic worldview
remains strong and well-entrenched. When it has been applied to the
undeniable mechanical aspects of the world, the results have been
impressive and often very important. Nothing in what is written here
should be taken to suggest that the quantitative and mechanical are
unimportant or, in themselves, harmful, and should be rejected. They
are abstractions useful for specific purposes. For their full and beneficent effect the mechanical and quantitative require a purposive and
qualitative context that they cannot provide for themselves. Without
such a context for guidance, the mechanistic view tends to provide its
own mistaken context and the dominant explanatory principle for all
existence, with disastrous consequences.

3. Consequences of the Mechanistic Assumptions

The harmful consequences of mechanistic assumptions have been
building in scope and intensity for the past three centuries. Now
they threaten the future not only of human society and culture, but also
of life itself on earth. It is crucial that human beings become aware of
these consequences and of what is at stake. In doing so, we are confronted
by a very bleak situation. It is easy to look away; it is tempting, and
almost irresistible, to fall into a kind of unconscious (albeit uneasy and
niggling) complacency, as though the "okay world" will continue.

It is a temptation, however, which anthroposophists, of all people, are
called to resist. Rudolf Steiner himself said: "We need to be awake and
alive for the sake of humanity. If Anthroposophy is to fulfill its purpose,
its prime task must be to rouse people and make them really wake up."[8]
He said this at the height of World War I, warning at the time that unless
people did wake up and strive to understand the nature of what was
happening, further catastrophes would follow. In light of the disasters that
have befallen humanity since, his warning remains as significant as when

he issued it. Now we stand at a point where the demand to awaken is more urgent than ever. It would be a daunting task to have to demonstrate that our situation today is any less perilous than in Rudolf Steiner's time.

To be asked to look unblinkingly at the full dimensions of our situation today might appear at first to be a counsel of despair born of a dead-end pessimism. Nevertheless, Rudolf Steiner himself spoke of the necessity at times, on one level, of a "justifiable pessimism." At the deepest level of our lives, he said, we should be neither optimists nor pessimists but do our work. But on the level of becoming aware, he said a certain pessimism is justifiable: "justifiable" if it "becomes a challenge to be awake and to try, whatever your place in life may be, to awaken souls so that the science of the spirit can send out its impulses."[9] Risking this justifiable pessimism, let us look at the situation the dominant assumptions of the modern mindset have helped create, assumptions that have worked to block the development of the science of the spirit.

3i. Fundamentalism for All

During the past half-century, religious fundamentalism, once largely underground in sectarian withdrawal, has emerged with a vengeance, and has been spreading worldwide. It would be a mistake, however, to see fundamentalism as only a religious phenomenon. To be sure, no religion has been immune. Every religion currently has its fundamentalist wings—Judaism, Christianity, Islam, but also Hinduism, Buddhism, Sikhism, and others, much to the surprise of many Westerners who have supposed Asian religions to be more gentle and tolerant than the admittedly aggressive Abrahamic religions. Beyond the religious fundamentalism, political, economic, and scientific fundamentalisms are also rampant. It appears that no group, association, or movement is immune to the fundamentalist temptation. How are we to understand this? What is the essence of fundamentalism as a social-cultural phenomenon? In what way is it connected with the dominant, mechanistic assumptions of the modern mindset?

Modern ways of knowing, limited as they are to the mechanistic and sense world, cannot deal with the nonsensory dimensions of human experience—meaning, values, and qualities—except to explain them away as surface epiphenomena of an underlying quantitative substratum. These non-sensory-spiritual realities, however, are the essence of human life, and they do not go away. They keep coming back, reasserting themselves. In the dominant modern view of knowledge, however, they cannot be known in any proper sense of the word; they can only be asserted arbitrarily and dogmatically, that is, fundamentalistically. The dominant modern, mechanistic assumptions make impossible a knowing of nonsensory realities that transcends social and cultural boundaries. Such a knowing could, in principle, be shared by all persons and so serve as a common foundation for cooperation and resolution of conflict. Without such a knowledge basis, however, religious, ethical, and aesthetic judgments are all rendered dogmatic and irrational. This holds equally for political, economic, and scientific, as well as for religious, assertions of ultimate ends and values. In short, fundamentalism is pervasive as a characteristic tendency of modern consciousness.

From this point of view, we can better understand one of the glaring ironies of religious fundamentalism, namely that it is largely a reaction against the corrosive acids of modernity and at the same time a prime expression of modernity. On the one hand, some fundamentalists have seen clearly that a mechanistic worldview is destructive of crucial human values and experience, and have felt keenly the loss entailed: the dissolution and scattering of community, the undermining of identity, the loss of meaning. All this fundamentalism strives to combat. On the other hand, fundamentalism can only wage this battle of resistance dogmatically and negatively because it has accepted the modern view that ultimate aims and values cannot be known. They can only be accepted and asserted dogmatically as given variously by religious scripture, tradition, cultural custom, group feeling, and so forth. The implementation of ultimate values, once given, can then be pursued by means of modern technology and technical reason. Many commentators have remarked on the embrace by almost all forms of religious fundamentalism of modern technology and their near-genius use of it: from hardware, such as cell phones, computers, and military technology, to the latest business and organizational management techniques. Thus we have the interesting picture of fundamentalists fighting the inroads of modernity and in the process often out-modernizing the modernists on their own ground.

In that the reaction against modernity becomes a major carrier of it, fundamentalism is subtly preempted, and in fact corrupted, from within.

Non-religious fundamentalisms—political, scientific, economic—are, of course, not combating the modern, mechanistic mindset for they have embraced and are frequently major promoters of it. In their own way, however, they are as fundamentalist as the religious fundamentalists whom they see as their archenemies. Unwittingly, their value assertions are just as arbitrary and irrational as those of the religious. All in the modern world who would affirm and advance value commitments that have no grounding in qualitative, imaginative, spiritual knowing have to do so dogmatically, drawing upon the givens of tradition, ideological commitments, emotions, convention, or power interests. In this light, modern liberals and conservatives, each advancing against the other their contrasting value claims, often have more in common with one another than either would like to admit.

Because of its dominant sense-bound and mechanistic assumptions regarding the acceptable method and content of knowledge, the modern world in general has a quintessentially fundamentalist character. The tragedy is that when values clash, as they inevitably do, the arbitrary assertion of ultimate values can only end in conflict. There is no underlying knowledge base in which a deeper unity can be sought. Religious and value conflicts, now virtually universal in scope, have also become quintessentially modern.

3ii. The Degradation of the Human Being and the Destruction of Nature

The great twentieth-century mathematician and philosopher, Alfred North Whitehead, once gave a description of the picture of nature presented by the mechanistic view of the universe: "Nature is a dull affair, soundless, scentless, colourless; merely the hurrying of material, endlessly, meaninglessly."[10] Subscribing to this view of the universe, many prominent scientists today affirm that their own scientific research reveals to us an ultimately meaningless, pointless world. The Harvard physicist, Steven Weinberg, has famously stated: "The more the universe seems comprehensible, the more it also seems pointless."[11] The biologist William Provine has written: "Our modern understanding of evolution implies that ultimate meaning in life is nonexistent."[12] The astronomer Sandra Faber has said, "the universe is completely pointless from a human perspective." And echoing the same thought, the Harvard astronomer Margaret Geller asks, "Why should the universe have a point? What point? It's just a physical system, what point is there?"[13] Many more similar statements from the highest ranks of the scientific community could be added. As one encounters these commanding nihilistic declarations, it is worth recalling Whitehead's wry comment: "Scientists animated by the purpose of proving that they are purposeless constitute an interesting subject for study."[14] But the irony here does not seem to shake the view of many leaders of the scientific community that ours is a meaningless world. Perhaps it is to their credit that at least they do not shrink from drawing the nihilistic consequences of their materialistic, mechanistic view.

These scientists are among the most influential of public figures. Science is the dominant modern faith and these scientists are its high priests, cultural icons for the whole of modern society. Their view of a totally meaningless, mechanistic world seeps into all aspects of modern society with profoundly negative effects. This nihilism offers no resistance to all those forces that work to corrupt and coarsen everyday life. It provides no support for affirming the realities of beauty, ethical ideals, and the responsible self. Nor does it offer any resources for recognizing and struggling with the depths of human existence—the human potential for good and evil, the mysteries of biography, the creativity of human imagination, the value of shared community and sacrifice for the other. About the only values—ideals, if they may be called that—supported by this nihilism are survival and self-aggrandizement in the struggle for survival.

In this view, the machine is regarded as clearly superior to the fallible, slow and limited, mortal human being. Increasingly we are inundated by proposals to "improve" the human being through genetic engineering, nanotechnology, and the creation of human-cybernetic machine hybrids. "Improve" in this context means to radically modify human nature. The hope is that the human being will no longer be subject to disease, death, and stupidity. There has even been the founding of a "World Transhumanist Association." Some scientists are eager to create a "transhuman," "posthuman," and "metahuman" state. While it remains doubtful whether this technological transcendence of the human being as envisaged can be achieved, this kind of thinking undercuts and trivializes all recognition of the depths of human life in all its misery, grandeur, and potential. And it offers no resistance at all to what Owen Barfield has called the possible creation of a "fantastically hideous world."[15]

Probably the most pressing consequence today of the mechanistic philosophy and its accompanying nihilism is that it offers no support for the protection and care of the earth. The emphasis on the machine parts and the absence of any sense of living wholeness simply provide permission for the relentless dismantling of nature. Erwin Chargaff, a noted biochemist and one of the few leading scientific critics of the modern scientist faith, has written:

> The over-fragmentation of the vision of nature . . . has created a Humpty-Dumpty world that must become increasingly unmanageable as more and more pieces are broken off. The wonderful, inconceivably intricate tapestry is being pulled out, torn up, and analyzed; and at the end even the memory of the design is lost and can no longer be recalled.[16]

As several observers of the earth situation have commented, "Nature doesn't exist anymore"—only bits and pieces, fragments, remain.

In addition to having direct, disastrous consequences, the view of nature as nothing but matter in motion also supports the exploitation and misuse of the earth through an unrestrained economism—the constant drive for unlimited economic growth and consumerism. The costs to the earth are now painfully apparent: The destruction of forests; the degrading of arable land; the pollution of lakes, rivers, and oceans; the depletion of fresh water sources; the mass extinction of living species; the world-wide collapse of fishing stocks—the list of destruction goes on alarmingly. The "Living Planet Report" by the World Wildlife Fund has recently concluded: "People are plundering the world's resources at a pace that outstrips the planet's capacity to sustain life."[17]

A special responsibility for this state of affairs rests with the people of the United States, who make up only six percent of the world's population and consume 30 to 40 percent of the world's resources. It is little comfort that India and China will soon share with America more and more of the responsibility for the pollution and destruction of the earth as the rate of their industrialization accelerates. The situation promises to worsen, and to do so very quickly. "Resource wars" over diminishing agricultural land, energy resources, and especially over fresh water are already being fought (as witnessed in the Middle East and Africa), and planning for more such wars worldwide has long been in process.

To add to all of this, if global warming and climate change come to pass as predicted by most of the world's experts, then all bets on the future are off.

We might think that this plundering of the earth is mainly due to thoughtlessness, greed, and general human cupidity. Certainly greed and thoughtlessness have always been with us, and in all ages have played major roles in the depredation of the earth. But the problem in our time goes much deeper than that, so long as nature is regarded as basically a dead, meaningless machine, as only matter in motion. Greed and thoughtlessness—and comfortable indifference—are all given a free hand as never before, within the doubly disastrous context of overpopulation and destructive technology. As long as nature is regarded as having no qualities—no inner life, no meaning, no living wholeness—taking it apart for our own immediate pleasure and economic advantage is obviously that much easier to justify.

A vivid example, much overlooked, of how a mechanistic view of life, social and cultural attitudes and greed, habit and complacency, powerful technology, and hardness of heart all come together and intertwine, is the treatment of animals by modern, industrial agriculture. Apart from the well-documented environmental degradation, communal decline, and spread of disease associated with the factory farming of animals—particularly pigs, cows, and poultry—the suffering of the animals themselves is almost never faced. Yet, daily our culture inflicts cruelty and suffering on millions of animals of an intensity hitherto unknown. The animals are defined as "units of production" and are treated accordingly as useful pieces of machinery without feelings. A pall of suffering of living, feeling creatures hangs over our modern culture, and most of us are complicit in it, if only through willful ignorance of what is taking place.

The suffering of these animals is one of the moral disasters of our time—obviously a startling claim amid all the many other horrendous, daily cruelties, but a true one nonetheless. The withholding of mercy to these fellow creatures bespeaks an appalling failure of imagination in thinking, a lack of empathy in feeling, and a weakness in moral willing. If it be said that the suffering of animals pales in importance in comparison to the horrid suffering of millions of human beings today, then it may be well to remember the words of Mahatma Gandhi: "The greatness of a nation and its moral progress can be judged by the way its animals are treated." This same lack of imagination, empathy, and moral determination stands as a barrier to the development of any powers of qualitative knowing.

A quantitative, mechanistic way of knowing can handle quantities and the machine aspects of the world with great efficacy, and, in its place, is very important. But the qualities of nature in and around us are disappearing—the qualities of life, meaning, beauty, and wholeness, the very qualities that have no place in our dominant conception of how and what we can know. What cannot be known was first thought to be secondary, then, unimportant, and, finally, non-existent.

In 1971, John Cobb, a leading American philosopher and theologian, wrote a book, acknowledged by many at the time to be a small classic on the state of the environment. It was entitled, *Is It Too Late?* Almost twenty years later, Cobb and a former World Bank economist collaborated on a book on global economics. By that time, near the conclusion of their book they had to write:

> Each passing year we see foreclosed happier possibilities for the future. The recognition of possibilities gone forever inspires us with a sense of urgency. Delay is costly to us and ever more to our descendants and to the other species with which we share the planet. It is already very late. It is hard to avoid bitterness about what might have been done and about the additional missed opportunities each day. It is hard to avoid resentment toward those who continue so successfully to block the needed changes.

> Yet there is hope. On a hotter planet, with lost deltas and shrunken coastlines, under a more dangerous sun, with less arable land, fewer species of living things, a legacy of poisonous wastes, and much

beauty irrevocably lost, there will still be the possibility that our children's children will learn at last to live as a community among communities. Perhaps they will learn also to forgive this generation its blind commitment to ever greater consumption. Perhaps they will even appreciate its belated efforts to leave them a planet still capable of supporting life in community.[18]

But now, still nearly another fifteen years later, Cobb has recently written again:

Viewing nature as a machine has led human beings to treat it that way. We are moving toward a crisis of global proportions, and our mechanistic vision deters us from taking the drastic steps needed to change direction.[19]

We don't know if there will be a global catastrophe; predicting the future is risky. Most of the experts failed to foresee the sudden collapse of the Soviet Union or the end of apartheid in South Africa. As one wag has commented, however: "Miracles are possible, but that's not where you puts your money." It would be blind and irresponsible to ignore the many warnings of impending global disaster—the latest and thus far most compelling being Al Gore's book and film, "An Inconvenient Truth." If we do avoid the catastrophe (or, more likely, catastrophes), it will only be because human beings learned in time to know and attend to the qualities of the world. If the catastrophes do come, and it may be sooner than later, it will be all the more important to have individuals and communities working together to develop and sustain through it all a living, knowledge-grasp of the qualities of life, meaning, beauty, and spirit—in ourselves and in the world. The whole of Rudolf Steiner's spiritual science is devoted to that end, and in a way that aims to have fundamental and specific implications for science, society, and culture. As far as the future of the earth is concerned, any meditative practice or path of spiritual development that does not have as a main goal the transformation of knowledge in science, society, and culture can only be irrelevant.

Steiner spoke of a "justifiable pessimism" at one level if it helps us to wake up and be alert. At a deeper level, however, as I noted earlier, he said we should be neither optimists nor pessimists, but do our work. In a lecture at the end of World War I, he said:

You will preeminently keep the following before your souls: "I am, in any case, called to look at everything without illusion; I must be neither pessimistic nor optimistic, so that forces may awaken in my soul which give me the power to aid the free development of the human being, to contribute to human progress in the place and situation where I am." Even if the faults and tragedies of the age are very visible to spiritual science, this should not be an incitement to pessimism or optimism, but rather as a call to an inner awakening so that independent work and the cultivation of right thinking will result. For above all things, adequate understanding is necessary. If only a sufficient number of people today were motivated to say, "We absolutely must have a better understanding of things," then everything else would follow.[20]

This is the beginning foundation for a healthy society and culture, and for the healing of an ailing earth.

Notes

1. David Ray Griffin, "Introduction to SUNY Series in Constructive Postmodern Thought," *Spirituality and Society: Postmodern Visions*, edited by David Ray Griffin (Albany, New York: State University of New York Press, 1988), ix-xii.

2. Rudolf Steiner, *The Fall of the Spirits of Darkness* (Bristol, U.K.: Rudolf Steiner Press, 1993), 203.

3. Rudolf Steiner, *The Mysteries of Light, of Space, and of the Earth* (New York: Anthroposophic Press, 1945), 69.

4. Rudolf Steiner, *The Anthroposophic Movement* (Bristol, U.K.: Rudolf Steiner Press, 1993), 103.

5. David Ray Griffin, *Religion and Scientific Naturalism: Overcoming the Conflicts* (Albany: State University of New York Press, 2000), 139.

6. Francis Crick, *The Astonishing Hypothesis: The Scientific Search for the Soul* (London and New York: Simon and Schuster, 1994), 3.

7. Quoted in Leon Kass, "The Moral Meaning of Genetic Technology," *Commentary* 108 (September 1999): 38.

8. Rudolf Steiner, *The Fall of the Spirits of Darkness, 16.*

9. Ibid., 21

10. Alfred North Whitehead, *Science and the Modern World* (New York: The Macmillan Company, 1950), 80.

11. Steven Weinberg, *The First Three Minutes* (New York: Basic Books, 1977), 144.

12. Quoted in Huston Smith, *Why Religion Matters* (San Francisco: Harper's, 2001), 37.

13. Faber and Geller quoted in John F. Haught, *God After Darwin: A Theology of Evolution* (Boulder, Colorado: Westview Press, 2000), 105.

14. Alfred North Whitehead, *The Function of Reason* (Boston: Beacon Press, 1968; originally 1929), 16.

15. Owen Barfield, *Saving the Appearances: A Study in Idolatry* (New York: Harcourt, Brace & World, n.d.), 146.

16. Erwin Chargaff, *Heraclitean Fire: Sketches from a Life before Nature* (New York: Rockefeller University Press, 1978), 55-56.

17. www.panda.org/news_facts/publications/key_publications/living_planet_report/_index.cfm.

18. John B. Cobb, Jr. and Herman E. Daly, *For the Common good* (Boston: Beacon Press, 1989), 399-400.

19. John Cobb, "Buddhism and the Natural Sciences," www.religion-online.org/showarticle.asp?title=2218.

20. Rudolf Steiner, *Social and Antisocial Forces* (Spring Valley, N.Y.: Mercury Press, 1982), 28.

Michael—Spirit of the Times

Georg Kühlewind

Michael wood relief by Thorn Zay

F or modern man, a name does not have the same significance as it once did. The fact that someone is called "Smith" or "Miller" no longer means that he is dealing in "iron" or "flour," as was the case in the past. Occasionally names do work back on their bearers, who adapt themselves to their names. (Laurence Sterne noticed this; we find a small passage about it in his strange novel *Tristram Shandy*.)

That the word by which a human being is called can alienate itself so far from its essence is caused by the evolution of consciousness towards nominalism. This development can occur because man is the only spiritual being with a natural body, i.e., an individual body that appears in the sense-perceptible world. As the capacity for spiritual perception vanishes, this body can be perceived and named independently from its inner being.

When after death man leaves his earthy nature behind, he enters a state of existence close to that of hierarchical beings; there is no part of him then, other than his essential being, that has any permanence as it did on earth. After death he is *only being*, that is, a word or name identical with his "doing," his "task," his "transformation." These are inadequate earthly words, yet their true meaning can be discovered through meditation. Speaking of this, Steiner says:

> Now try to imagine that what man is expressing, what is flowing into the fleeting word, would be a "self-uttering" of the human being, its essence and its revelation at the same time—then you find the way in which human beings meet each other in the middle between death and new birth, distinguishing their own being and revealing themselves. Word meets another word, the articulated

word encounters the articulated word, an inwardly enlivened word meets the inwardly enlivened word. The human beings themselves are the words, and their sounding-together is the symphony of the articulated Word-being. In this sphere human beings live together without untransparency; they are truly living with one another, and one word, which is one human being, merges with the other word, the other human being.

Here the karmic connections are formed which continue to work into the next life on earth; they manifest themselves in such a way that the human beings feel sympathy and antipathy as it were, when they meet and encounter one another. This feeling is a reflection of the way in which human beings have addressed themselves in the spiritual world, in the middle between death and new birth. This is how we spoke with the other, we, being speech ourselves. How we now find ourselves on the earth is merely a shadowy reflection of this feeling."[1]

Like man after death in the spiritual world, the angel-beings also have nothing besides their essences, nothing that could be named. They *are* their *being*-word throughout, all name, meaning nothing but their being alone—identical with their task and mission, their "wording"—when they appear as visions to the human being. Thus Gabriel is identical with his words spoken to Mary in the scene of the Annunciation, words that become human words in the intuition of the Virgin. He is this intuition: his whole being is the message.

We must take seriously the *names* of the angels and archangels—if we were only capable of understanding them! The words have lost their original and primal meaning for us. Only in meditation can one sometimes enter their inner sanctum and have ignited a tiny spark of understanding: Gabriel—"God's Hero"; Raphael—"God Heals"; Uriel—"God's Light"; Samael—"God Listens"; Orifiel—"Light from God's Mouth"; Azael—"God's Power." Who dares to look behind the sound of the word? Its glaring surface forces away the inexperienced. The name of the 'Spirit of the Times,' Michael, is a question: "Who is as God?"and only in English or German is the mediating copula 'is' expressed. With the exception of a dubious tradition found in a hymn from the Rigvedas, Michael is the only divinity who carries a question for a name. Today this name seems to be very near to the human being, in its form of a question as well as in its meaning.

Compared to a statement, a question is transparent; it is a quest; it means 'to be on the way'. This is implicit in the name of Michael, and is oriented towards God. It is an eternal quest, directed at the highest aim. One can avoid a human question, but cannot avoid a question that is *being*— such a mighty being. He who meets *that* question is forced by the might of an archangel and archai: "Reflect on yourself! Know thyself!" Therefore, this being's name, this name-being, is itself the weapon of its "bearer"—again an inadequate human expression—against the two adversary forces, his archenemies. Only when imagined in a human form does he bear weapons: lance or sword. But these images themselves show how unearthly is his use of *these* weapons; his gaze is never directed at the adversary or to his weapon, in spite of which he finds and meets them with surety. It is his *glance*, his questioning searching look, that is his true weapon. He himself is the question that cannot be evaded.

Therefore, the arrogant spirit who fancies himself God falls from heaven, pierced by the Michael-question. His darkness, his darkening, is illumined. Against the spirit of the lie, the question *Michael* works differently; it aims at the *word*, the Logos, the word that is misused in lying. For it is the Logos who is as God—"And God was the Word" (John 1.1). This is the answer to the Michael-question; that is in his deep connection with the Logos. The answer causes the darkest enemy to fall from his heaven, a realm made up of the misused word. This is the victory of Michael.

> over that which is not silent in silence,
> over the mocking evil;
> to un-do himself without a trace,
> the word was shown to him.[2]

By his name, which is a question, the Spirit of the Times depicts the pressing, necessary human step. Never has such a stride been as urgent nor as possible as today. The period of innocence during which primal wisdom was given without question is followed by the period of doubt, when questioning is the only means to find a way out. Steiner stated it thus:

> And those who announced the call for the Holy Grail wanted it to

sound within the darksome soul already as a dawning of freedom. They did not want to take man's freedom, nor impose something. Man was to ask questions. He was to ask from the depths of his soul-being for the miracles of the Grail.[3]

> But these [disciples of the Grail] were especially admonished that they had to ask; that the time of the evolution of mankind had come, where man, if he did not ask questions, if he remained passive, could not come to an experience of selfhood, unless he seek from within himself the impulse of truth.[4]

Behind the saying "God is dead" is the experience that the Godhead is now silent: Without the contribution of questioning on the part of man, the Godhead is no longer given. *Man* must begin: "ask, seek and knock."[5] Then Michael, the Spirit of the Times, the divinity which is waiting for *his* step, *his* beginning, can offer help.

The administrator of cosmic intelligence—as he is described by Steiner in the Michael-letters—is the "power from which the thoughts of things are flowing."[6] This refers to the things of nature, not man-made objects. Today the human consciousness does not grasp the ideas of the phenomena of nature, because they are created in such manner that no word-language can express them totally. The "thoughts" of the things of nature, their true names, have been "spoken" in the non-sounding primal language, the language of creation. Every name in a human language contains only a part of the primal Word. The cosmic intelligence lives above all languages, which participate in it, take "part" in it. This explains why the Spirit of the Times is now standing above language and folk. Steiner says:

> Michael strictly refuses everything that is separating: for instance, in the human languages. As long as one is only clothing one's discoveries in the language, not raising them into thought, as long as this is the case one cannot come near to Michael … In fact we have today the strongest spiritual battle in this direction; for a great part of mankind thoughts are non-existent, because people are thinking in words. But thinking in words is not the way to Michael. Michael, one can approach only if one reaches through the words to true inner experience of the sprit, not depending on words. This, in fact, is the secret of modern initiation: to overcome the words in order to experience

the spirit. This does not impinge on the experience of the beauty of language, for when one is no longer thinking in a language, one begins to experience language, it begins to stream out as an element of sensation, begins to stream within oneself.[7]

In his silent way of expectation, the Spirit of the Times directs the human striving upwards, above the languages, in the direction of the creative, "wordless word."[8] In relation to the word of a language, the *wordless word* is to be found in the opposite direction, that of *abstract* thinking, which has separated itself from the language.

From this wordless *but all the more wording* sphere, the adversaries were thrown upon the earth into the zone of everyday consciousness. One might find this disconcerting: is man in his weakness supposed to fight against forces which are nevertheless to be overcome by someone like Michael? The insight should emerge that here on earth the power of the adversaries can only unfold through forces which were stolen from the human being himself, through man's highest creative forces which were not used, cherished, exercised, and not even glimpsed. If man is aware of this fact he will, in freedom, begin the path of schooling the consciousness, and by this *first step* he will ascend to the first heaven of the imaginative sphere purified by Michael and liberated of the adversaries: In this heaven he can then receive the instruction of the Spirit of the Times, and purified by practice, unite his forces with the impulses of Michael. Strengthened in this way man can neutralize the adversary forces on the earth by withdrawing his own forces from them. This, in the interest of the *upwards striving human being*, is the purpose of the fall of the Spirits of Darkness.

In his living consciousness man can pass from concept to concept, from thought to thought, from word to word. He has at his disposal, in a free and still unstructured form, that which has already adopted a shape in the concepts of thoughts and words. If man pictures the latter as vessels like vases, glasses, jugs, then man has the ability to pour his free-flowing intelligence in and out of these vessel-forms.

But is it really *his* intelligence? For in waking consciousness he does not accompany this process to its point of destination, where the still-unformed fluid immerses itself into the forms. His consciousness awakens only after the intelligence has already formulated itself into an idea, a thought formulated through words: the moment preceding this remains super-conscious. This is the very point of transition where, in thinking, the body apparatus (or mirror) is touched and seized by the pure thinking, and where subtle magic occurs when something new is being thought. Then in a homeopathic manner the living power of thinking annihilates the structures which it finds in the brain, thereby repressing the *biological* life of the brain.[9]   This is the point at which the bearer-less form—not written into substance, the pure constellation (one should call it "pure information")—receives bearer and substance. At some point every seal's form passes from a purely spiritual pictorial existence into brass, gold, or any other substance.

The pure word-less form of an idea, and its preceding determination of the living-fluid intelligence, usually remain super-conscious. This is still in the hands of Michael.   He is the administrator of the cosmic intelligence, which he hands over to the human being.   In earlier epochs the ideas were formed by the Spirit of the Times Himself and given through inspiration to the chosen ones among mankind: they communicated these ideas to the rest of mankind.   When mankind comes of age the ideas must be formed by the human being himself—and in principle everyone is chosen to receive the inspiration through his own work, to take his own step upwards.   For the inspiration no longer descends the whole way to the consciousness of the earth.

The moment is not *watched* when the living intelligence assumes its form, when it passes over from the administration of the Spirit of the Times into the responsibility of man.   It is man's task, and he has the possibility to accompany this transition consciously; but it happens very rarely.   It is during the unobserved moment when in the transition to man that the intelligence can be diverted and distorted by the adversary forces and through *subconscious* inspiration formed into ideas which are hostile and detrimental to mankind; this is what often happens.   Today it is the task of man to be able to receive the intelligence as *light of thought* before it becomes *thought*: that it passes from the hand of Michael, accompanied by the consciousness of man, into his own hands. This is how we have to read the silence, the waiting, Michael's preparing of the space for the spiritual striving of man. The unimposing manner of leaving man free is his mighty spiritual gesture: *the silent waiting invitation to action, to personal initiative.*

If the emergence of the idea in the human consciousness is secured as an undistorted continuation of the living cosmic intelligence-by the human being meeting it—until it reaches its point of destination, then the root of the idea appears as well, its feeling and willing in resonance. This leads the seeker to the "Thinking of the Heart."   If man starts to look at the phenomena of nature not as things, things without meaning beyond themselves, then he begins to consider them as *signs* which are to be read. This is also the beginning of the elevation and transformation of the feeling of reality—that which normally accompanies the act of perceiving—into reading and cognizing Feeling and Willing. This is the beginning of a new epoch in the history of the earth.

—*Translated by Friedemann Schwarzkopf*

Notes

1. Rudolf Steiner, "Supersensible Man" (Nov. 14, 1923, GA 321.90; London 1961).

2. R.M. Rilke, "Zueignung" ("Dedication"), in *Werke, Auswahl in Zwei Baenden* (Frankfurt: Insel-Verlag, 1957), p. 340.

3. Rudolf Steiner, "The Materialistic Impulse of Knowledge and It's Significance for the Whole Evolution of Mankind," trans. by M. Cotterell (Apr. 16, 1921, GA 204-89).

4. Rudolf Steiner (Apr. 17, 1921, GA 204.99).

5. Matthew 7.7.

6. Rudolf Steiner, "Anthroposophical Leading Thoughts," (Aug. 17, 1924, GA 26.60; London 1973).

7. Rudolf Steiner, "Rosicrucianism and Modern Initiation" (Jan. 13, 1924, in English, GA 233a; also Mai 5 and 6,   1918, in German, GA 271; London 1965). See also "Sprache und Sprachgeist" (GA 36.296).

8. Rudolf Steiner, "Man in the Light of Occultism, Theosophy and Philosophy" (Oct. 1, 1920, GA 322; June 4 and 5, 1912, GA 137; London 1964).

9. Rudolf Steiner, *Philosophy of Freedom*, 1918 edition, Chapters 9 and 12.

Toward Meeting Evil with Consciousness

Adeline Bianchi

An event in the outer world can evoke an image which is branded into the soul to become a prod for attention. Such an image for me was found in pictures of the faces of family members of the victims of serial killer Robert Alton Harris when he was executed in 1992. Their faces expressed joyful ecstasy, a triumphant celebration of the extinction of the life of a man who had himself been brutalized from his earliest years. It was this haunting image that I carried to a social science conference at which Manicheism was one of the themes. Mani lived in the third century and founded Manicheism out of his insights into the Christ impulse. He developed a great following throughout the Middle East and even into China. Much of his teaching concerned the interplay of good and evil. It is the Manichean legend, briefly related as follows, that I wish to offer as the imagination that is the connecting tissue for this article:

> While the Powers of Darkness were chasing and devouring one another in a wild rage, they arrived one day at the borders of their territory. Here they glimpsed a few beams of the Kingdom of Light and were so struck by the splendid sight that they decided to relinquish their quarrels among themselves and took counsel together as to how they could gain mastery over the Good which they had just seen for the first time and of which they formerly had no notion. … When the Father of Light became aware that Darkness was about to attack his holy Domain, He held counsel to decide on a punishment. But, as He had no means of punishment—there being no evil in the House of God—He sent forth a soul force to mingle with the materialized Kingdom of Darkness. This introduced a leaven, a ferment which produced a chaotic, whirling dance which contained a new element, that is, death. Thus the Kingdom of Darkness consumed itself.[1]

This event was considered the origin of human beings, as the force which streamed out from the Father of Light was called the Mother of Life from whom came the archetypal man. Clothed in five pure elements—light, fire, wind, water and earth—archetypal man descended to earth to counter darkness. The force from God is called the Universal, or World, Soul by Mani and in the Gnostic tradition, the Heavenly Mother or Holy Spirit.[2]

> The profound thought which lies in this is that the kingdom of darkness has to be overcome by the kingdom of light, not by means of punishment, but through mildness; not by resisting evil, but by uniting with it in order to redeem evil as such. Because a part of the light enters into evil, the evil itself is overcome.[3]

The inspiring images of this legend added to the disturbing one arising out of the execution of Robert Alton Harris gave substance to a motivation to work toward expanding my consciousness of the nature of evil.

When we look out into the world, or the world invades our lives via the media, we see an epidemic of evil—ethnic cleansing in Bosnia, clans slaughtering clans in Africa, senseless shootings close to home, and a more silent evil, toxic dumping, that endangers human life and the earth itself. Indeed it appears that evil is escalating. When I was a child schools were safe places; the innocence of childhood had not been blighted by the evil of children killing children. Ghost stories could conjure up fearful imaginations but the real world was generally experienced as offering a measure of security. In spite of the flower children's songs of love and the '60s, increasing rage begets atrocities in ever greater measure. It is enough to dull our sensibilities and cause us to wish to find a safe haven; however, the truth is that there is no place to hide. These thoughts enlarged the question of evil which continued to haunt me somewhat like a Greek chorus ever in the background.

The question of evil became even more compelling when I had an opportunity to travel to eastern Germany. After we visited Weimar, my traveling companion suggested that as we had just seen where German idealism flourished with Goethe and Schiller, we ought to visit nearby Buchenwald, one of the infamous Nazi concentration camps, as a contrast. We set out the next morning, traveling along a road into the mountains which gave a sense of going to a beautiful vacation retreat.

When we arrived at Buchenwald we saw a vast area enclosed with a barbed fence beyond which was thick, green forest-land. All the barracks where the prisoners had lived had been demolished and each site covered with black rubble. The spaces between were brown dirt and gravel road-ways. There was not a single plant anywhere, not even a weed. The barrenness contrasted sharply with the woodlands outside. The only remaining buildings were a barracks that had been converted into a museum in a distant corner and at the far right the crematorium. I could not let myself imagine the unspeakable horror that lived in that atmos-phere. My reaction was numbness. At one point there flashed into my memory the reports of the massacre at My Lai in Vietnam—a message that evil is carried by all people.

The crematorium powerfully evoked the suffering of so many innocents, including children, yet I felt only greater paralysis. The museum depicts the history of the camp since the mid-1930s, portraying barrack life with many enlarged photographs of emaciated prisoners—images we have all seen on television or in newspapers and magazines. After we left and stood in the midst of all the barrenness outside, I reflected on the last message at the exit of the museum which read, "I shall not rest until every Nazi criminal is punished." I believe the quotation was from Simon Wiesenthal, the man who dedicated his life to hunting Nazi war criminals. Then came the thought, seemingly from nowhere, if we meet evil and do not begin to transform it in some measure, do we not become infected and, therefore, susceptible to committing that evil, at least to some degree? Could this be a spiritual law?

Since that unforgettable visit to Buchenwald, other questions presented themselves:

> *How does evil work on the human being?*
> *What is the meaning of evil?*
> *How can we meet evil with greater consciousness?*

I began to look to spiritual science for insights and a deeper understand-ing of the Manichean legend.

To the question, "How does evil work on the human being?" Rudolf Steiner indicates that evil attacks the soul forces—our thinking, feeling and willing. Our thinking renounces the spirit. This brings to mind the persecutions, torture and murder of untold numbers of people by the Stalin regime under a communism which denied the spirit in human nature. In our feeling our soul becomes a void. This can relate to the mass killer who has no remorse, who seems devoid of feeling, or our computerized war machine whereby an individual impersonally releases a smart bomb, or not-so-smart bomb, which kills civilian populations with anonymity, without feeling. In our willing we become dedicated to the powers opposing human evolution. An example is Nazi Germany's drive to exterminate several groups of people, failing to recognize our need, as part of evolution, to strive for a sense of our common humanity, to perceive the individual beyond race, gender and other externals, to affirm the higher self in the other. How much work we all have to do to transform our thinking, feeling and willing!

If it is true that "in no age was it granted to human beings to do so much wrong as in this, since in none could one sin more deeply against the inner mission of the time,"[4] then the mystery of good and evil is central to our age. Pursuing this line of thought may shed light on the question of the meaning of evil.

Long before human beings existed in the form we know today, the earth was imbued with wisdom as a gift from the spiritual world. The earth and its creatures are actually permeated with wisdom, evidenced by the 'knowing' of the spider in spinning her miraculous web and in the wisdom-filled structure of the thigh bone which can carry the greatest possible mass of weight with the employment of the least material and force. None of this was invented by the human being. Human intellectual achievements are a discovery of wisdom already embedded in the earth. Now human beings have come 'of age' as it were and are ready to be responsible for the task of this age: that is, to use the gift of wisdom to create the cosmos of love, evolving love from the most elementary stage to its highest. However, just as wisdom was born out of error (yes, the gods did have failed experiments), love is born out of conflict. The highest love requires freedom. It must be manifested totally out of free deeds. But freedom comes out of choice; without choice one is not free. Here then is the necessity for evil in the evolutionary process. We must be able to choose between good and evil.[5]

Now we are confronted with the question of how to meet evil. Is it simply a matter of choosing good and ignoring evil? Steiner speaks of the Essenes, who through practices of purification lived a life of purity removed from the world. He recounts that as Jesus of Nazareth was passing through the gate to the Essene community, He saw two figures He recognized as Lucifer and Ahriman fleeing from the sanctity of the Essene monastery. The question, "whither are they fleeing?" pierced deeply into His soul.[6]

It was with this dilemma of how to respond to evil that I encountered Sergei Prokofieff's book, *The Occult Significance of Forgiveness*, in which he relates the concentration camp experience of Simon Wiesenthal, the man I believe was quoted at Buchenwald. The story was so compelling that I looked for Wiesenthal's book, *The Sunflower*, the first half of which relates his concentration camp experience in detail.[7]

Wiesenthal tells of living with death and torture as an everyday reality. One day when he was on a work detail disposing waste material at a hospital for Nazi soldiers, a nurse took him to a room where a Nazi SS trooper lay on his deathbed swaddled in bandages so that only his eyes, lips and nose were visible. From this dying man, no more than 21 years old, Wiesenthal heard his confession.

In his early youth he had entered the Hitler youth movement and then volunteered to join the SS. Shortly afterwards he was sent to the eastern front. The crime that the dying man wanted to impart to the Jewish prisoner occurred in a Ukrainian town. Upon abandoning the town, the Russians had mined many of the houses and streets. Explosions occurred and several German soldiers were killed or wounded. Vengeance was not long in coming. Between 150 and 200 Jewish prisoners, who were drawn from the non-military population of the town, including many women, children and the elderly, were driven into a small building, where tanks of gasoline had been placed in the upper story. The doors of the building were firmly shut and the SS soldiers (including the young man narrating the story) were ordered to ignite the gasoline by shooting the tanks and then to shoot anyone who tried to escape from the blazing inferno by jumping from a window.

One image in particular was engraved in the memory of the dying man—that of a man holding a child in his arms. His clothes already alight, he covered the child's eyes and jumped from the window. The mother jumped immediately after them. "We opened fire, but I shall never forget this family, especially the child." With these words the dying man ended the story of this terrible event.

The SS subdivision to which the Nazi soldier belonged was sent south where there was heavy fighting. The memory of the crime gave him no peace. "It was some time before I became aware of how much guilt I had incurred," he went on to say. "I wasn't born a murderer. I have made myself a murderer." Then he described what happened in the midst of the heavy fighting in the south.

> Suddenly I stood still. Something was approaching me. My hands, which were holding a rifle with a fixed bayonet, began to tremble and I saw with total clarity the *burning* family coming toward me and I thought, "no, I won't shoot them a second time." Then a grenade exploded beside me and I lost consciousness. When I came to my senses I was in the hospital and realized I was blind, my face mutilated and the upper part of my body consisted of nothing but wounds. It was a miracle that I was still alive. I was as good as dead.

The immense physical sufferings were nothing in comparison with the unendurable moral torments and pangs of remorse he experienced day and night. Finally after a pause, the dying man uttered the following words:

> I know that what I have told you is terrible. In the long nights that I have spent waiting for death I have had ever and again the need to speak with a Jew about it… and ask his forgiveness. … I know that what I am asking is almost too much for you. But without an answer I cannot die in peace.

After these last words there was silence. Then without a word Simon Wiesenthal left the room.

Obviously this experience was etched deeply into Wiesenthal's soul unresolved, for he carried it for 20 years and then wrote a book about it. He asked a number of individuals—theologians, philosophers, educators, writers—to comment on his leaving the dying SS soldier without a word of forgiveness. The second half of the book is composed of these commentaries, which are an extraordinary sharing of moral struggles with evil and forgiveness. Most of them concentrated on the question whether we can forgive and also the role of remorse, recompense and retribution. I would like to share excerpts from a few that resonate with what we find in Rudolf Steiner's work.

Roger Ikor, French Author: "The most tragic side of the drama is that by not forgiving, one opens up the way for one's own lack of humanity. Simon Wisenthal could doubtlessly have acted in no other way than he did; but in so doing, he was denying his suppliant his individual existence. He was then, morally speaking, committing the very crime committed by Nazism or come to that, of any form of racialism. His only excuse in the last instance is that of revenge."

James Parkes, British theologian: "I am absolutely convinced that the young Nazi, in his repentance, goes into the next life seeking those whom he so terribly wronged, and seeing those who very likely without repentance, wrought the wrong with him. … That alone reconciles on the one hand the infinite beauty and richness of creation and, on the other, the immeasurable horror of evil of which the holocaust is certainly the most appalling example."

Manes Sperber, French author: "The two peoples (Jews and Germans) are bound together in startling fashion by the terrible events, just as the young SS man on his deathbed and the prisoner Wiesenthal were bound together. And Wiesenthal will be bound until his dying day. Though their misdeeds and their sufferings may make it enormously difficult to live together in lasting peace, yet nothing now can separate them from each other."

John Oesterreicher, Catholic theologian: "In reconciling one human being to another, or man to God, the one who forgives restores, even though it may seem only on a small scale, the integrity of being. 'Only on a small scale' implies a surface view, referring as it does to appearance:

At their deepest reality, all events exist on a great, a world scale. Viewed philosophically, the whole is present in all its parts. Thus it can be said that the history of each person—undoubtedly part of world history—is world history. In other words, anything a man or woman does, even in secret, touches, more than that, shapes the whole of human kind."

These commentaries reveal in varying degrees of clarity a consciousness of some of the principles of spiritual science which bring light to the darkness of evil. One is holding an image of the human being as body, soul and spirit and recognizing that this image applies to all human beings. Another is that evil has meaning and purpose in the larger view of the evolution of humanity. The third concerns the destiny connections we have with each other and the role of karma as a balancing or redemption of evil not as punishment. In Steiner's *The Gospel of St. John*, there is a revealing passage:

> …The Christ brings to expression in the highest sense, the idea of karma, the karmic law. For when anyone fully understands the idea of karma, he will understand it in this Christian sense. It means that no man should set himself up as a judge of the inner soul of another human being. Unless the idea of karma has been understood in this way, it has not been grasped in its deepest significance. When one man judges another, the one is always placing the other under the compulsion of his own ego. However, if a person really believes in the "I am" in the Christian sense, he will not judge. He will say, "I know that karma is the great adjuster. Whatever you may have done, I do not judge it."[8]

Can we trace an evolutionary development of how evil is met? We recognize that 'an eye for an eye' is an Old Testament concept. However, a friend, who is knowledgeable about the Jewish tradition, pointed out that we are indebted to the wise men of the Hebrews who developed this doctrine because before the principle of 'an eye for an eye' was accepted, total realization was the rule. If a wrong was done by an individual from a neighboring village, the whole village was punished. We would like to think we have moved beyond both of these modes, yet in capital punishment we see that 'an eye for an eye' prevails, and in war aggressive action often causes a regression to retaliation with bombing of large civilian populations.

What is required to get beyond modes of revenge? To move forward requires strengthening our capacities of true interest and understanding of our fellow human beings. This would mean directing interest toward the biography of the perpetrator of an evil deed as well as toward that of the victim.

Sergei Prokofieff calls our attention to a form of forgiveness that is a severe test for the soul—that of 'forgiveness for one's destiny' when one is beset with an incurable illness or other desperate life condition. He reminds us that this destiny is the result of a previous karmic decision made by one's higher ego as a spirit-enabling trial. The process of true forgiveness involves an experience of inner powerlessness when one renounces the desire for vengeance but one is not yet able to rise to one's higher ego. A resurrection from this experience of powerlessness can lead to meeting the Christ.[9]

Steiner gives indications of elements we need to develop if evil is to be transformed in such a way that our Consciousness Soul will be strengthened to prepare for the Spirit Self. He speaks of a process that will mature only in future epochs. First he directs our attention, not to the evil actions in society but to evil tendencies—even to "ignoring the consequences of these tendencies which are manifested more or less in a particular individual and turn our attention to the evil tendencies themselves."[10] In response to the question, "in which human beings are these tendencies active in our age?," he states that evil tendencies are subconsciously present in all human beings.

> There is not a crime in the calendar to which every human being, insofar as he belongs to this age, is not subconsciously prone. … Man must assimilate these forces of evil which are operative in the universe. By so doing he implants in his being the seed which enables him to experience consciously the life of the spirit. The purpose of these forces of evil which are perverted by the social order is to enable man to break through to the life of the level of the Consciousness Soul. … Mutual concern for each other must grow and develop especially in four domains:

First, through art we have the possibility of seeing our fellow human beings in a different light. At present we have no real understanding of our neighbors. Although almost every branch of artistic creation and appreciation is at a low ebb, art embodies something that leads to a deeper and more concrete understanding of the human being—an understanding of his picture nature through which we can experience the spiritual archetype of the human being. We can have an inner experience of others in the warmth that penetrates our life forces and an enhanced interest will develop between human beings.

Second is the need to develop a capacity to feel, to sense in our neighbor his relationship to the angels, archangels and archai. This will emerge out of an elevation of language so that by listening to what a human being says we will hear the soul through the words and this will lead to a different community life.

Third, we will need to be able to experience inwardly the emotional reactions of others through our own breathing. "According to the changing rhythm of our respiration we shall feel the kind of man with whom we are dealing."

Fourth, when human beings belong to a community of their own volition, in willing something in common, we will have the inner experience of 'digesting' one another.[11]

Prokofieff speaks of forgiveness as a socially formative power.

An awareness of the necessity for forgiveness in our world makes us truly "brothers of Christ." This true forgiveness has, as one of its chief prerequisites, a real "understanding" and, through this, an—albeit only partial—sharing in the destiny of the other person (who may be guilty before us or before others who are, perhaps not even known to us), thus making it a part of one's own destiny. … Here we have the true source of the new social community, the future community of the Holy Spirit, the Spirit who, as the substance of cosmic love, streamed down upon the community of the first Apostles on the day of Pentecost. And through what Christ has brought down from the spiritual heights, this web is to bear the character of a reflection of the order that prevails in heaven, that is, the karma of the individual is united with the karma of the whole in accordance with the order that prevails in the spiritual world, not in a random fashion but in such a way that the organism of the community becomes a reflection of the order that prevails in heaven. ...[12]

To return to the question that appeared before me at Buchenwald—Is it a spiritual law that when we meet evil, if we seek only vengeance and do not begin to transform it, that we become infected with the evil or it activates our own evil tendencies? Do we not see how old grievances, old judgments and the inability to forgive feed the passions for conflict and brutality? How much of our current tragic situation comes from not recognizing the laws of the universe? Steiner observed that "A person can be born and die today without having any inkling of the fact that laws are working themselves out in us, and that everything we do is governed by the laws of the universe. The whole of present-day life is wasted because people do not know that they have to live according to laws."[13]

We share a common task to struggle with the questions of the meaning of evil, how evil works in our soul, how we can become aware of the spiritual laws pertaining to evil and how we can bring more consciousness to our encounters with evil. This exploration has turned my attention from the evil out in the world to the evil tendencies I carry within. The challenge is how can I replace judgment and the desire 'to get even' with mildness and the warmth of interest and forgiveness.

Arthur Zajonc, in his book *Catching the Light*, describes the miracle of the candle—how "the bright yellow cone that spreads its gentle radiance is due to tiny glowing embers of unburned carbon. Cold, it is one of the blackest of substances, the most vulgar material, but when hot, soot becomes beautifully luminous. ..." Quoting poet Gaston Bachelard, he adds, "... The most vulgar material of all produces light. It purifies itself in the very act of giving off light. Evil is the nourisher of good. In the flame, the philosopher encounters a 'model phenomenon,' a cosmic phenomenon, a model of humanization."[14]

This gives new meaning to the saying, "It is better to light one small candle than to curse the darkness."

Notes

1. Rudolf Steiner, *The Temple Legend, pp. 358-359.*

2. Ibid.

3. Ibid. p. 63

4. Rudolf Steiner, *Ancient Myths: Their Meaning and Connection with Evolution,* p. 57.

5. Rudolf Steiner, *The Origin of Evil*, Lecture Berlin, 22 November 1906.

6. Rudolf Steiner, *The Fifth Gospel*, pp. 78-79.

7. Simon Wiesenthal, *The Sunflower.*

8. Rudolf Steiner, "*The Gospel of St. John*, p. 120.

9. Sergei O. Prokofieff, *The Occult Significance of Forgiveness*, pp. 86-88.

10. Rudolf Steiner, *From Symptom to Reality to Modern History*, p. 117.

11. Ibid., pp. 118-126.

12. Sergei O. Prokofieff, *The Occult Significance of Forgiveness*, pp. 96-100.

13. Rudolf Steiner, *The Temple Legend*, p. 140.

14. Arthur Zajonc, *Catching the Light*, Chapter 9.

Joseph Beuys—The Protest Against Materialism's Deformed Image of Man

Diether Rudloff

On January 23 of this year [1986] one of the most controversial figures of German art, Joseph Beuys, 64, died. He first became famous in 1962 for his sculptural "Happenings" that fought against the static forms of traditional sculpture. From 1961 to 1972 he was professor of sculpture at the Düsseldorf Academy. Turning more and more to social political arenas he founded the German Student Party in 1967, the Organization for Direct Democracy in 1971, and finally, in 1973, he founded the Free International University for Creativity and Interdisciplinary Research. But to appreciate the sources of his work, whether artistic, political, or social, one must understand the impulses and experiences out of which he strove. To this end we reprint, with the kind permission of Verlag Urachhaus, excerpts from Diether Rudloff's book, Unvollendete Schöpfung: Künstler im Zwanzigsten Jahrhundert (Unfinished Creation: Artists in the Twentieth Century).

From Space to Time

Nobody who seriously tries to come to terms with the contemporary art scene can avoid the phenomenon of Joseph Beuys. His life and his work, both of which create a greater than usual public stir, are the boulder against which the most contradictory opinions about the meaning of art crash. With his unceasing stinging assertions, sometimes even provocations, Beuys dominates the current art dialogue in an almost magical way, as before him perhaps only Picasso did, so that the very mention of his name precludes indifference on anybody's part. His artifacts and "Happenings" have veered too far away from the ordinary conception of art not to arouse by sheer necessity the most vehement emotions pro and con. His followers implacably confront their embittered opponents in the fray. It would appear from this that any objective consideration is out of the question. Nevertheless, one thing is certain: in his activities, which range ever more daringly into areas of life hardly, if ever before, touched by art, Joseph Beuys meets somewhere along the line the decisive point where the *Zeitgeist* is.

This is reason enough for a final judgment to be hardly possible, as is the case with many phenomena of contemporary art. The difficulties threatening an unprejudiced understanding mount formidably. On the one hand, Beuys' body of work appears entangled in quite subjective biographical phenomena to which the viewer cannot easily gain access. His work can appear as an attempt to control his personal destiny by magical means taken to a manic degree. It appears as the outward projection of a merely personal process which not only leads away from art but even jeopardizes communication with the external world. But we must not be deceived by this nor let ourselves be satisfied with our first impression. For it is important to question more deeply and to focus on the overall historical, as well as spiritual, context from which the heavily encoded statements of Beuys have emerged. A solid basis for doing this is handily offered by the universal approach of Anthroposophy which, to be sure, takes its departure from the scholarly question of epistemology but then always decisively transforms that into a quite individual question of beliefs. Just how one approaches Beuys is inseparable from one's own state of consciousness, from the individual's spiritual needs. In this light the judgments often reveal more about those making them than they do about Beuys.

Since the period of Expressionism it has been a general maxim that, as far as the art of the 20th century goes, there is no longer a generally binding concept of what art is, nor must each new stylistic movement, each artist, and each work be explained out of their own specific backgrounds. The old normative aesthetics is dead at last, and with it the rules about what constituted a work of art. For it regarded the reality of art with no fresh unprejudiced eye, but rather judged according to rigid statutes. What we now need is an interpretive aesthetics such as was developed at the turn of the 20th century by Rudolf Steiner in a Goetheanistic, spiritual way. For since the Renaissance every work of art has been the product of an individual human being, and its most

Beuys' artistic action event 1965

valuable aspect, through which it achieves its highest perfection, has been the unique quality of the artist who produced it, which appears only once in the world. Thus a work of art becomes more significant the more it has in it what is not repeated, what is present in one specific person only. Therefore Steiner can no longer recognize general laws for art nor an ever-valid aesthetics, for every work demands its own aesthetics. For such an aesthetics, every modern work is a new revelation. It judges in each critique according to new rules, just as the true genius creates his every work according to new individual rules.

Thus in the 20th century, in the Age of Michael, everything can be art. Everything is worthy of representation—to the extent that every form and every content are an adequate expression of the individual creative power of an artist. Conversely, every form and content become immediately untruthful and unconvincing if this power does not manifest itself. To quote from Rudolf Steiner's notebooks: "Painting is worthless if one does not sense the human being in it even in the way the most amorphous spot is painted—otherwise it is inhuman." For this reason the art of the 20th century challenges the viewer in a previously unknown way; for it demands of him the utmost activity, his fully engaged, personal participation. A further phenomenon: art today is no longer valuable in itself but is often only a means to an end. It becomes an opportunity for trying out new powers, such as a new sensitivity of the soul or a new spiritual freedom, or it can become a means of healing for the individual alienated from himself. From space to time—so can this development of art be characterized. The material result, the finished artifact as such, is no longer the goal. The essential factor is increasingly the path that leads to it, the creative act. The emphasis then shifts from the stationary work to the active process.

JOSEPH BEUYS ◆ *63*

But the final result of this is the end of art in the traditional sense.

In this development Joseph Beuys may be reckoned one of the leading spirits. It is therefore not surprising that his efforts encounter a complete lack of understanding and rejection by those who apply the old standards and adhere to the traditional conception of art. Beuys' art appears rooted in four large areas of his experience: (1) his childhood experiences, which determine to an unusual degree the form and content of his performances and artifacts; (2) his wartime experiences as a Stuka pilot, particularly in Russia and the Crimea; (3) his encounter with Anthroposophy; (4) the deep anchoring of his art in the tradition of German Romanticism, especially of Novalis (there are traces of this throughout his work)—all of which seems rather astonishing since Beuys radically tosses tradition overboard. Still, there is a quotation which might have been written with Beuys in mind, a surprising confirmation of this orientation—except that it was written 175 years ago in a letter from the north German Romantic painter Philip Runge (dated 19 June 1803) to his brother Daniel:

> The extensive interest that is now fashionable to show for all branches of *science* and for art limits the whole human species and does a pretty good job of negating all art, because everything has either the same degree of interest or else none at all. Art will have to be really despised and considered useless before it can become something again, or it will have to be applied to everything in a quite defective way. We wish in vain for the public to understand us properly. An understanding of individuals is the only thing we can obtain and is the only thing that keeps us going. In the big soul, on the other hand, we drown along with all our individuality in the end, so that we ourselves still see a big clear green mass good for cooling and growing cold and so we leave the world, unnoticed by the least of the least.

These sentences seem to include everything that constitutes the greater spiritual background, as well as the individual elements, of Beuys' art. In the wake of the 18th century era of the Enlightenment, in which Kant's influence more than anything else helped to secure the triumph of science, technology, and industry, the ancient unity of western spiritual life was to break apart; not only were faith and knowledge, art and science, and art and life now unrelated to one another, but they bitterly fought one another. The 19th and 20th centuries appear even more "Kanted." Kant's nominalism wins the upper hand in all spheres of life, reducing the concept of science to a one-dimensional rationalism and thereby breaking off all connection with man, nature, and the cosmos, as well as cutting art off from the wellsprings of life. Art was thus debased to a noncommittal aesthetic game far removed from the needs of life, that is, removed to a decorative feature of Sundays and holidays.

All this Joseph Beuys assaults bitterly, and every work, every one of his performances, is a symbol of his profound protest.

Social Sculpture: Vision of a Future Art

The work and philosophy of Beuys find their crowning achievement in his idea of social sculpture—"soziale Plastik"—which points beyond a merely aesthetically experienced art. Sculpture to him is synonymous with the human being altogether.

> Plastic art, in my opinion, is a concept that is not understood deeply enough. Sculpture is so often still conceived of very much in terms of an outward effect. In the earlier days of Europe that was not the case. In Greece, for example, the human being as a whole was an expression of sculpture itself. The Greek human being considered his own body formed in relation to sculpture. It was not only an ornamental need, it was the model for what the Greek pictured as a human form, the guide for the way a human being properly ought to be formed. [235]

For Beuys, plastic art has no real sense unless *it works upon the development of human consciousness.* Thus in 1969 he developed his plastic theory, which derives from Rudolf Steiner's idea of threefold organization. For Beuys, plastic art arises out of various elements. In the first place there is the will life—flowing, undifferentiated—into which something altogether opposite engages itself, something that the human being also has in his thinking:

> Here already we have two opposite principles leading to a plastic work—the chaotic will element and the formal thought element— meeting and coming to terms with one another. Between the two

there are a great many differentiated intermediate concepts, particularly what is called the rhythmic element, which clearly comes from feeling. And thus I see it as the actual mean, balancing the extremes. So schematically, we now have three elements. To be sure, there are certainly many more. … and that, I would say, is my plastic theory—"theory" in quotation marks here, because to me it is not a theory at all, but a reality. [236]

In the new future art of social sculpture, a *plastic of cold* arises wherever alienation and isolation hold sway among men. Communication, brotherhood, understanding, and love, on the other hand, awaken what Beuys calls the *plastic of warmth*. To him, conscious human thinking is of itself a plastic art, and so it is that each individual human being can become a sculptor and modeler of the social organism, capable of molding it in a human form. Beuys reaches to the stars. He knows once again that art has a significance pointing to the most distant future ages. And this, once again, places him in the great cultural tradition of German Idealism, of the Romantic Movement, and makes him a true descendant of Fichte, Schelling, and most especially of Novalis. For it was the latter who spoke of the *Kunstmensch*—the "art-man"—the one who would be able to *romanticize* all things in the most various spheres of life. Trade, agriculture, even soldiery, would be conducted as an art, thus transforming the entire social organism into an image of the "art-man." [237]

In a future age—still aeons removed from us, to be sure—the human being will no longer have to paint pictures, create sculptures, write poems, compose music, or build buildings. Novalis' demand will have become reality: we ourselves will have become the work of art, the musical instrument, and so we shall be able to unite with others in the social art, the architecture of the Heavenly Jerusalem. For we shall be able to generate inner pictures whose color and warmth will radiate outwards again, transforming and enlivening a world that has grayed, cooled, and lost its life.

This is something that Piet Mondrian knew, and Joseph Beuys knows it as well in his own way. This is why he so decisively rejects a shortsighted view of his works and processes, which would see him as interested only in the grey, the desolate, and the sullied. No, he says, it is just through presenting the grayness that he wishes to call up a color-filled world as a responsive image in the viewer:

> Thus: to provoke, as it were, a luminous world, a clear, bright, in
> some circumstances a supersensible, spiritual world, through some-
> thing that looks totally different—precisely through a counterimage.
> For afterimages or counterimages can only be generated by not doing
> what is already present, but by doing something that is
> present as a counterimage—always in a counterimage process. [240]

Thus in the work of Joseph Beuys we can see a path leading across a
threshold, an altogether individual, perhaps an extremely narrow, path.
It is an attempt—and not always without danger—to forge ahead, out
of the cul-de-sac, out of the nothingness of our present, into the reality
of a spiritual world. Only Joseph Beuys himself, out of the conditions
of his own destiny, is able to go to this path in this way. But the attempt
to go at all is a Michaelic one, which can awaken other human beings
and give them the courage to start out on the path themselves and
become creative.

—*Translated by J. Leonard Benson and Peter Luborsky*

The Survival of Architecture

Rex Raab, A.R.I.B.A.

In 1960, Sir William Holford, the newly elected President of the Royal Institute of British Architects, made the following timely admission at an official conference: "In occasional dark moments of despair, I wonder whether architecture itself will survive the battle for its life which is being waged by this generation and the next. I do not refer to building, nor to 'building development,' as it is called these days, but to architecture that lifts the heart and delights the eye, that appreciates the better qualities of its own age—including its advances in scientific thought—and is therefore likely to be remembered, and preserved, by future ages."

This is an utterance worth dwelling upon.

Former ages never failed to bring forth modes of building which, in retrospect, are seen to have been indispensable and beneficent lawgivers to the community—the pyramid, a man-made mountain peak planted between river and desert, rousing the slave from a world of dream; the temple poised on its rocky promontory, indwelled by the god, assurance to the peasant that all is well in the land; the cathedral, piled up towards the sky by the craft of hands soon to be folded in prayer. Such works are tangible inspiration. They are concrete embodiments of Goethe's adage about "the manifestation of secret laws of nature, which, without art, would forever remain concealed."

What, then, is the peculiarity of the twentieth century, that the very foundations of architecture, in the opinion of one of its recognized exponents, are in serious danger? Do Holford's words imply a valid indictment against half a century of "modern architecture?" Or are we merely being asked to witness a personal confession of failure? Has the immense building activity of recent decades failed to find a true foundation assuring its sound future development? What is the architecture of our day, if not an expression of advances in scientific thought? Or is something other than applied empirical science intended here?

The pursuit of architecture fit to survive will not lose itself in questions, however apposite these may be. It will move on to do just what Holford recommends, "appreciate the better qualities of its own age—including its advances in scientific thought." It will hasten to do what it has so long postponed; it will have recourse to the results of modern spiritual science. In Rudolf Steiner's work those better qualities and those advances find direct expression.

Steiner's answers to the question of the survival of architecture were first and foremost practical answers in reinforced concrete and timber and glass; timely answers, when only the skirmish in the battle for architecture was on, during the first, second and third decades of the present century; answers just in the nick of time calculated to save the architectural endeavors of Western society from needless groping down barren paths. Let there be no mistake!—the survival of architecture now depends upon the extent to which those responsible–architects, engineers, clients and contractors—are prepared to revise their formulae for building. Art has a serious mission to perform. Architecture must once more be made into an indispensable factor in human life.

It was the "goldsmith" Brunelleschi whose constructive genius unfolded in the face of the uncompleted cathedral of Florence to create the first great dome of the Renaissance; and the "painter" Michelangelo who alone knew how to take the colossal task of St. Peter's in hand. Goethe was the last who was gifted by nature with such universal scope, and felt as much at home designing columns and cornices as writing a play or presiding at a cabinet meeting, and did it better than the "professionals."

Rudolf Steiner's universality must be understood differently. It is in accordance with the needs of the new age. Admittedly his initial studies were shaped with a view to his becoming a civil engineer, and did stand him in good stead when he later became associated with architecture in practice. But his tireless search and efforts were primarily directed to the justification of spiritual experience before the strictest tribunal of scientific thought; and it was not before these efforts were crowned by the creation

of a spiritual scientific method capable
of being communicated to others, that
he felt entitled to turn to practical
application in other walks of life. That
architecture was not overlooked in the
process, however, but remained an
object of wakeful attention (which
could well put us architects to shame!)

Second Goetheanum

may be gathered from his confession in later life that he had suffered many
a sleepless night in his student days over the problem of the origin of the
Corinthian capital! Let no one suppose that this concern was a mere
matter of detail. It was nothing less than the defense of architecture as an
art against the attacks being launched by that utilitarian interpretation of
its origin which has not yet been cast overboard.—The first effective
weapon in the battle for architecture is the strengthening of our knowledge
of its origin and office through spiritual research. The second is actual
artistic practice in the light of the knowledge so won.

The chief fruit of Rudolf Steiner's architectural work was the first
"Goetheanum," built in Dornach on the western slopes of the Swiss Jura
near Basel. Its story, which has been told often enough in picture and
word, is fraught with struggle, setback, victory, tragedy, renewed hope,
and undaunted effort, and bears all the signs of being part of the battle
for architecture. Closer reference to this remarkable work of building
genius will only be made in order to lend an otherwise brief analysis the
necessary concreteness.

Characteristic of the Goetheanum is the capacity of its designer to shape
each detail in accordance with the whole. The first beginnings of such a
conscious procedure in art may be traced back to Munich in 1907, when
Rudolf Steiner was afforded his first opportunity to create in architectural
terms. His design of a sequence of columns whose capitals are without
precedent has become the basis for a new and living architecture. Each
capital is a distinct stage in an evolution of form from a simple beginning through greater complexity to a "higher simplicity" or maturity at
the end, the whole comprising an indivisible unity, much as the seven
colors are united in wisdom and beauty in the rainbow. Just as the

Doric, Ionic and Corinthian Orders of Architecture are clearly manifestations of the inner evolution of the Greek spirit and at the same time supremely appropriate building forms, so our times have witnessed in these seven basic Goetheanum columns a similarly happy and even more coherent architectural embodiment of those forces which support and guide *every* cycle of evolution.

Questions put to him by architects and engineers made it possible for Rudolf Steiner to enlarge on his ideas for the incorporation of these pillars in an interior where they would perform their rightful office as supports and form an environment conducive to the pursuit of modern spiritual knowledge. For tasks of a different order these particular designs would of course be inappropriate, and other, suitable forms would have to be found.

Since the Goetheanum was to house a stage as well as an auditorium, the original plan for a single elliptical interior was given up and a far more significant architectural conception took its place—whereby the Munich project had to be adapted to the exposed position in Dornach. It is to the interior, harmoniously and consistently executed in every detail, that we should turn in order to receive the full architectural message of this building.

Two rotundas, incomplete on plan, and of unequal diameter, crowned by hemispherical cupolas, intersected to form an interior space with the stage opening at their junction. The original columns now formed an arcade bounding the area occupied by the seating in the auditorium beneath the larger dome—fourteen columns in all; whereas twelve further columns, whose bases assumed the form of imposing seats, surrounded the stage area beneath the smaller dome. The final pair of columns in the east, flanking a wide and lofty arch on the axis of symmetry, was destined to frame a colossal work of sculpture some thirty feet in height as the culminating feature of the whole interior. Stage and auditorium, though unequal in size, thus possessed equal architectural value.

The total internal length was about a hundred and fifty feet, the internal diameter of the larger rotunda a hundred and ten feet, its maximum internal height some eighty feet, and the seating capacity about nine hundred. Owing to the slope of the auditorium towards the stage, the columns progressively increased in length and girth, from the first pair framing the entry beneath the musicians' gallery in the west, which attained a height of thirty-four feet, to the pair supporting the proscenium arch, reaching forty-five feet, so that each successive column appeared to contain its precursor within itself, thus heightening the metamorphosis from one arch to the next.

The impression of immensity native to architecture was here achieved by more subtle means than mere size. Those who knew the first Goetheanum are unanimous in declaring that the forms of its interior seemed to be in a constant state of expansion, so that the beholder was enclosed in a material sense only. The treatment of the painted domes, the architraves and pillars carved in relief, and the engraved glass windows, made the wall "spiritually transparent" for one endowed with artistic sensibility.

Architecture, sculpture, painting, music—the whole building was "frozen music"—poetry, drama, and eurythmy (that art of movement called into being by Rudolf Steiner's insight into the deeper laws of the human body, which, at the opposite pole, also inform architecture)—all the arts met under the hospitable roof, the twin domes, of this House of Speech, as its creator liked to call it. Architecture became a "mother of the arts" once more. The effect of this veritable choral concourse was that each separate artistic element became transfigured, and infused with a new vigor. The art of building was here revealed in its archetype: the structural laws of the human physical body—the chest, with its pillar-like supports, and crowned by its doming brow. What is only too commonly a bare skeleton was here suffused with warmth from the heart. Even the word architecture points to its origin in the human breast. An ark of a new covenant was actually built in the full publicity of modern times, to become the inspirer of a new generation of artificers. If this is taken to heart, there is no need for even "occasional dark moments of despair."

Space here precludes entering into a discussion of the various timbers and other materials employed in the construction of the first Goetheanum. Suffice it to say that new art-forms gave rise to their concomitant techniques.

The deep sense of responsibility, unparalleled enthusiasm, personal sacrifice and practical effort of what now seems like a mere handful of supporters reflecting Rudolf Steiner's own attitude, succeeded in a few months in getting this considerable undertaking sufficiently far advanced before the outbreak of war in 1914 to secure the further progress of work. Anyone who has been afforded access to the working drawings and models which arose at the time, and has followed the dates carefully, comparing them with progress on the site, will hardly have escaped a feeling of incredulity mixed with warm admiration at the speed with which completely revolutionary—or rather, evolutionary—artistic conceptions were mastered and realized in practice. The movement for a healthy spiritual life untrammeled by the dictates of state or finance, which here created for itself a world headquarters in free Switzerland, may justifiably look with pride to the fact that, whilst the thunder of the guns in neighboring Alsace rolled over the hillsides, individual representatives of nearly twenty of the warring peoples were engaged on this constructive labor of peace, in which was to stand the great sculptural likeness of the Representative of Humanity.

The first Goetheanum was burned to the ground on New Year's Eve, 1922-3-the victim of human jealousy.

But a new Goetheanum arose like a Phoenix from the ashes of the old, larger and better adapted to its modern task, and this time entirely of reinforced concrete. Not merely a monument to the memory of its precursor, but a telling work in its own right, fashioned out of a sure feeling for the qualities and possibilities of the new material, the present Goetheanum has stood the test of the intervening decades and will continue to offer a challenge that is at the same time encouragement to all those concerned about the survival of architecture.

The difference between the two buildings is more apparent than real, for each is informed by the same active principle, in which interior and exterior, the whole and the parts, bear an organic, not a passive, relationship to each other. Indeed, the exterior of the later work represents a step forward, possessing greater strength and unity of expression.

"I have learned something," Rudolf Steiner said in this regard.

His artistry in this case lies in the handling of a dominant twofold formal theme—trapezium-shaped auditorium and rectangular stage block—developed "musically" right into the details and brought into movement through the powerful counterpoint of mass and concavity. Mediating between those two extremes is a pair of lofty piers, one on each side of the building, at the artistic, not geometric midpoint. The duality is thus resolved, the laws of architecture satisfied. A threefold composition speaks throughout length, breadth and height, relating the beholder to the dimensions of space—the earth, the sky, and the surrounding landscape.

The loyalty which led Steiner to dedicate this center of cultural activity to the Goethean spirit can here be understood from the strictly architectural side. Goethe was the first to state clearly that architecture arises out of the interplay of three distinct elements: base or foundation; wall or pillar (to him but two aspects of the same thing); and roof or crowning feature. A self-evident truth? Apparently not.

Various ancillary buildings in the vicinity of the main edifice in Dornach also stem to a greater or lesser degree from Rudolf Steiner's formative hand: dwelling houses, studios, a characteristic boiler house, a transformer house ... but it was a source of disappointment to him that conditions did not allow of a more consistent town planning development. His particular concern, however, was to stimulate others in a fruitful line of approach to modern problems, rather than self-expression at all costs. In this—his ability to bring out the creative powers in his fellows—lies his significance for future generations.

If applied physical science has been successful in promoting remarkable advances in building construction and the technical services, applied spiritual science is able to restore the balance, disclosing the relationship of architecture to the human being and the world order, and setting up challenging new goals, in the realization of which both artistic talent and technical invention are equally important. The field of utilitarian building in particular has scarcely yet been explored by the architect. "A school building is an artistically treated utilitarian structure" is one of Rudolf Steiner's many hints—that is, something midway between a temple of learning and a factory for ginning in knowledge! And he himself, on his own admission, would have been as readily prepared to tackle a railway station or a bank building as a center for spiritual activity in science and art, for in such tasks the innate capacity and need of the creative spirit to enter into and transform the material world is seen to best advantage.

In this sense, monuments are being erected to Rudolf Steiner all over the world—wherever, in the solution of their tasks great and small, grateful architects and craftsmen look to his example for their inspiration. Even in modest attempts, that may not always be successful, they can say to themselves, "I have learned something," and move on to the next attempt, never indulging in more than they can answer for, but firmly grounded on the living bedrock of an architecture in the service of man rather than the machine. The conviction grows that even imperfection, if it is a product of genuine striving, holds out more promise for the future than easily attainable mechanical perfection.

In an age when so much is heard about launching man into space—mechanically, buildings based on the planet Earth should bring men to their senses. The only salutary way of launching man into space is through architecture, the spatial art! Firm stance, erect posture, sure tread, free movement, clear gesture, calm brow—architectural environment can be the silent but eloquent, severe but benevolent instructor in how to become worthy of the instrument of the human body.

Not only did Rudolf Steiner set up the highest known goals for architecture, but he was also able to initiate the first practical steps towards their attainment. One evening, when the machines had been stopped after a day's work, he once spoke these words to his active collaborators on a great building project—architects, engineers, sculptors, artists in many fields, artisans, and others dedicated to building:

> My dear friends, however much men may ponder on external ways and means of ridding the world of crime and antisocial tendencies—true healing, the turning of evil into good, will, in the future, depend upon the extent to which true art is able to instill a spiritual fluid into human souls and human hearts, so that—once they are harmoniously surrounded by the forms of a sculptural architecture—should they be untruthfully inclined, they will cease to lie; should they have violent natures, they will cease to disturb the peace of their fellow men. Buildings will begin to speak. They will speak a language of which men still have little inkling.

The next morning his hearers—and he himself, no doubt—were up on the scaffolding again, bringing that divinely inspired language a little nearer to their fellow men.

The Spiritual Heart of Service: Self-Development and the Thinking Heart

Cornelius Pietzner

It is with the heart that one sees rightly; what is essential is invisible to the eye.

Antoine de Saint Exupery, The Little Prince

I am done with great things and big things, great institutions and big successes, and I am for those tiny molecular moral forces that work from individual to individual, creeping through the crannies of the world like so many rootlets, or like the capillary oozing of water, yet which, if you give them time, will rend the hardest monuments of man's pride.

William James

Service has been essential for humankind since the beginning of time. The main point of this presentation is to suggest that the very heart of service is itself spiritual. Obviously there are numerous aspects to service. Yet at the core of service there is not just an outer activity or gesture, but an accompanying inner, non-visible action. Often spiritual things, by their nature, are less dense, less palpable than material phenomena. In some ways, they can be elusive, fleeting, and indirect. This makes it difficult to describe the heart of service, since the heart is something spiritual involving our inner being, our life of morality, and our soul life.

I work with developmentally disabled individuals in intentional, spiritually-based communities. I have often found that persons with certain types of disabilities need to be approached in special ways. Sensitivity to this can make for more effective, accessible and lasting relationships. For example, I have known individuals with autism who seem to respond better over time with a less direct, less "in your face" approach. People with the so-called Fragile-X Syndrome (often confused in earlier years with autism) also respond better to a more elliptical, indirect approach. Non-direct eye contact, the deliberate "suppression" of a strong personality (if it is your own), asking leading questions rather than making command statements—all these methods allow the delicate, yet beautiful personality of the person with Fragile-X to shine forth. In other words, the less we become, the more can they be. This is an attribute we are neither accustomed to nor necessarily comfortable with. In our social engagements we are unpracticed in making less of ourselves in order that the other may be more themselves. Indeed, we often take the opposite approach as a way of "getting ahead."

The willingness to dampen down one's own personal expressions and needs is connected to another tantalizing yet frustrating paradox. Particularly in human relationships, the more we want to do, or perform a service, the more, too, can we erode the dignity of those we perform the service for or do it to. The capacity of helping without in any way diminishing the other is a quality to strive towards. How can we reduce the charity aspect of service (helping the poor and unfortunate) and increase the parity of service; we help each other—you can teach me through your illness, your need, something that I need to know about myself, the world etc? Like the first issue, this aspect of mutuality in service calls on the inner participation and conscious awareness of the "service provider" to change something within him/herself so as not simply to render a service (do a good deed), but be willing to change *oneself* in the process. The willingness to change oneself, to work consciously on one's own being, points, I believe, to the heart of service.

Service, when truly rendered, does as much, if not more, to the initiator, the one ostensibly providing the service, as it does to the recipient. This is because service works back into the initiator in a way that suggests and even necessitates a conscious step in the inner life. This conscious step is a spiritual happening. In other words, the true nature of service has the characteristic that it changes you, inwardly. This change can be even greater than the change made upon the recipient of your service. Martin Luther King Jr. said: "All men are caught in an inescapable network of mutuality, tied in a single garment of destiny. Whatever affects one directly affects all indirectly. I can never be what I ought to be until you are what you ought to be, and you can never be what you ought to be until I am what I ought to be."

If service does not change you, if you are unable to become inwardly mobile, inwardly alert and sensitive, I suggest that the service you are performing is a form of charity and is eluding the core and heart of what service can be. If it doesn't touch you it remains outside of you and somehow separate.

Ultimately, when this inner dimension of service is active, we are truly serving each other. This dimension is a spiritual one. It is, seemingly, not outwardly connected to the "discharge" of the service activity

Photo © Copyright, Camphill Village USA

itself. When we heal or become involved in such work we place ourselves on a path of self-transformation. We become vulnerable. Voluntary vulnerability in the face of meeting another person, doing a task, helping someone, allows us to create a space in which the other one can enter us, can be met by us, and where we can meet them. This essential, non-judgmental inner gazing, is a kind of gentle soul assimilation. It is reminiscent of the statement of Martin Buber who said, "All real living is meeting."

Dr. König, the founder of the international Camphill movement which works with people with developmental disabilities in intentional communities, states something similar when he describes, "Only the help from man to man—the encounter of Ego with Ego—the becoming aware of the other man's individuality without entering into his creed, world conception or political affiliations, but simply the meeting eye-to-eye of two persons, creates that curative education which counters, in a healing way, the threat to our innermost humanity. ... The curative educational attitude comes about only there where a new kind of humility begins to grow in the heart which recognizes the brother in everyone that carries a human countenance."

Creating an inner space in your heart for the other's being to live, to grow and flower can perhaps be thought of in connection to the Christian saying: "Not I, but Christ in me." This already indicates a willingness to reduce one's own intentionality and persona, one's own purposeful will, and be receptive to another force or agent to work within one. I have sometimes thought to go a step further: "Not I, but Christ in *you*." This relates to the creation of a living mythos or mythology that we create, hold and inwardly cultivate on behalf of the other one. Naturally, one could substitute other words for this; "Not I, but the spirit in you." One does not need to be bound by the Christian ethic. Such concepts actually represent a methodology for the inner conduct of service. There will be and should be a spectrum of such methodologies, insights and alternatives.

A related and equally challenging point is creating a spiritual or inner morphology for such an ethic. There is considerable focus today on the concept of emotional intelligence, and of imbuing our cognition with feeling. Increasingly we recognize that pure intelligence is one-sided. The attempt to hold and develop a thought (say over three days), adds qualities and dimensions to the thought that originally did not exist. It is as if the thought generates additional attributes—for example, moral and social dimensions. The thought seems to "ripen." This and other such exercises are instructive and sobering. They can make us realize how careful we might be with our thoughts, especially those we deem important. There is value in becoming conscious of and thinking about thinking itself.

However, there is a difference in trying to develop conscious sensing capacities around emotion, or, I would prefer to say, the heart. How do we make the heart into a thinking organ of perception? Instead of bringing our feelings up into our head, how can we bring a level of cognition or knowing into our heart? This seems to me to be a key question related to the "heart of service." Intuitions can be cultivated and worked with to become a clear and reliable instrument of cognition and perception. Clairvoyant faculties are already something else.

In anthroposophical psychology, there are essentially two opposite modalities for the "kernel of consciousness" or the higher ego (the inner self) to operate and manifest. One is called the "central ego," or central self, connected to the head (nerve/sense function). This functions spiritually, and provides us with the easiest and more common access to the realm of the spirit. The other modality, quite to the contrary, works unconsciously into our will or intention system, through the limbs and extremities. These two "systems" create poles—the head/nerve/sense pole, where conscious-ness most readily resides, and the limb/metabolic pole where our will forces (which are relatively unconscious) work and are active. The former works from within out (from the brain, centrifugal), the latter works from without in, (centripetal movement) ultimately "resting" in the skeletal system. These two great systems are regulated by our "rhythmic" system, primarily through the beat of our heart and lungs. It is here within the ebb and flow of our rhythmic life that the heart moderates, modulates and har-monizes these opposite poles of our cognitive processes. The rhythmical heart and lung system is neither fully conscious (like in the head), nor fully unconscious (like with the will forces or the limb system), but is dreamy and only somewhat conscious. Of course, we are aware of our feelings, but to a less conscious degree than of our thinking process. However, we can develop this rhythmic system with care. We can also develop a special consciousness of it, which can allow it to speak to us in its own subtle lan-guage. It can become a tool and a guide, like a pressure-point of awareness.

Typically, brain-centered knowledge (which we often refer to as "head knowledge") takes very little time to acquire. A tremendous amount of complex information can be assimilated rapidly, at a relatively young age. This is different for knowledge related to the heart. This takes much longer to acquire—often a lifetime. Sometimes we can call this kind of knowledge wisdom. Yet wisdom is comprehensive and applicable to many situations. It is possible to develop the capacities of what could be called the "thinking heart" which relate to specific situations and circumstances. Nevertheless, to do even this requires a focused and cultivated patience not normally associated with the regular cognitive process. The process of sup-porting the transformation from head knowledge to heart knowledge is aided through the second element of service which I described above-cre-ating an inner room or space for another's being to live within us. As Dr. König describes for the work with special needs individuals: "We must learn to recognize ourselves as curative teachers in such a way that we are not only the guides but simultaneously the guided ones, not only the teachers, but at the same moment also the pupils."

The creation of this room or inner space is molded out of fundamental and genuine human interest. This interest, not based on particular sympathies or antipathies, serves as a kind of yeast or leaven—the active ingredient in this inner alchemy. This "heart-room" represents a new architecture and a new kind of construct. It becomes a formative element in creating space, in which the being of the other can live, can manifest. The activity of creating this space out of interest serves as an informing agent on the heart. Interest in the other serves as a builder of knowledge. Over time it can ripen into heart cognition. The thinking heart begins to become active. It imparts, albeit slowly, information. The beat of the blood has an invisible echo which is a silent counterpart. It emits a new kind of sensing, a new kind of knowledge. The human being, the "service provider," undergoes a subtle, yet fundamental and gentle process of self-transformation.

This process can become evident to those who observe and are interested in such phenomena. This becomes a basis for self-knowledge and inner transformation. Anyone genuinely interested can develop the inner tools of perception to notice such developments and changes.

In conclusion, the true heart of service is spiritual. There are distinct and clear inner phenomena that belong to the essential elements of service activity: they can be worked with and developed as characteristics and attributes. They belong to our realm of inner landscape and process of self-transformation.

There are other elements, also of an inner kind, that could be joined with those I have attempted to outline. For example, and only to suggest one other direction, it has been pointed out by many in the service field, that each area of activity, each field of interest, each ailment or illness, each sector or area contains its own meaning, its own message, its own teaching and its own being. There is a tremendous potential embodied in such an observation. However, it goes beyond the scope of this article to explore more than one or two of the inner dimensions of service.

Ultimately service is a powerful teaching, and those who are engaged in this work can attest to the far greater gifts that we receive than those we could possibly offer.

Working Together as an Aspect of Inner Development

Christopher Schaefer

With each passing decade human relationships of all kinds are becoming more difficult. Whether in the home or at work, misunderstandings, conflicts, and violence are increasing. How can we understand this development in supposedly civilized cultures?

Rudolf Steiner offered an historical perspective on this question which is, I think, of vital importance for the present and the future. In a series of lectures on social and antisocial forces in the human being, he suggested that people today would lose their social instincts, becoming more individualized, more self-conscious, and more antisocial.[1] He gave an apt picture for this which we can painfully experience every day: the image—"a hermit wandering through the world," a hermit who sees and speaks to others, but is fundamentally isolated and alone.[2]

Credence is lent to Steiner's view by the development of psychology. A hundred years ago there were few, if any, books on motivation, communication, leadership, conflict, and relationships; nor was there the interesting assortment of psychological bestsellers available at bookstands today. If something is not an issue, is not experienced as a problem, then I believe it is also not discussed and written about. A century ago human relationships were not a burning issue, but it is clear that they have become so today.

While we can already see the destructive consequences of the loss of social instincts, Steiner suggests that the antisocial forces in the human being will grow stronger in the next one thousand years.

It is the antisocial forces which require development in this time, for consciousness to be present. It would not be possible for mankind in the present to accomplish its task if just these antisocial forces did not become ever more powerful; they are indeed the pillars on which personal independence rests. At present, humanity has no idea how much more powerful antisocial impulses must become, right on until the 30th century.[3]

This prospect is, at the least, daunting for anyone concerned with the future of social life.

What then can be done to balance this evolutionary trend in human consciousness—to limit the tendencies toward social disintegration resulting from a heightened individual consciousness? Steiner indicates a variety of measures including the further development and spread of spiritual science, the fostering of a new kind of social understanding, and the creation of new social forms and structures which connect people to life and to each other.

It is this last point which I want to explore further in this essay. How do new social forms and structures, which many people are struggling to create, balance the inner antisocial forces of the human being? How do such structures work within the human soul?

It is clear from Steiner's work that by new social forms he not only means the threefold social order, but all social arrangements which challenge the human being inwardly and connect people consciously.[4] Such arrangements or social forms include income communities, long-term relationships including marriage, and all organizational forms in which people experience their interdependence. It is crucial in such new social forms that individuals feel jointly responsible for initiatives, that they are in some sense involved as equals, and that interdependence is acknowledged.

If we now look at how new social arrangements work as a balancing force within the individual soul, one of the more obvious aspects is their ability to bring out antisocial nature to consciousness. If we pay careful attention to our thought life when listening to another, we can notice that we selectively listen to what we agree or disagree with and then busily formulate a response. Observed more closely, we can see the quality of doubt, of critical intelligence directed at the thoughts of others.

If we observe our feelings, we can notice that our relationships are colored by a sea of sympathies and antipathies. There are some people in a working group whom I naturally like, agree with, and enjoy, and others with whom I have difficulty, no matter what they do. These likes and dislikes are not only the basis for judgments about others, but often also the basis of far-reaching decisions. Yet such feelings are usually quite unreliable, as they tend to say more about what we like or don't like about ourselves than anything objective about the other. Rudolf Steiner portrays these natural likes and dislikes as the greatest enemies of true social life since they block the development of real interest between people, hindering the search for a deeper, conscious understanding of karmic relationships.[5] The picture which has sometimes come to my mind regarding these forces of sympathy and antipathy is that they give rise to a butterfly collector mentality in us—they tempt us to categorize and then pin people to particular images. Once done it is impossible for anyone to escape—"Tom is always late, isn't he?"—and we needn't actually concern ourselves with individuals anymore. They are, after all, already categorized in our private collection.

If we observe our behavior, our intentions, something of our will in a group, we can quickly notice that when we get our way we are pleased, gracious, even open, but when we do not we react in a variety of negative ways. At this more subtle and less conscious level of the soul a certain selfishness and egotism reigns, even when couched in terms of wanting what is good for others or for the community. Marjorie Spock discusses this issue at some length in her important article, "Reflections on Community Building," and appropriately cites Christian Morgenstern:

> The lamb-vulture is a bird far-famed;
> The vulture-lamb is here first named
> It doesn't say baa, it doesn't say boo
> It just gobbles you up while embracing you.[6]

Through working with others we can come to recognize these three fundamental antisocial forces in our soul:

- – doubt and criticism in our thought life
- – sympathy and antipathy in our feeling life
- – egotism and selfishness in our will life

While these three soul forces can lead us to greater self-consciousness they also block a genuine meeting with others.

Knowing about our antisocial nature is of course not adequate—it must be repeatedly experienced and ultimately *accepted* if we are even to consider to future transformation. For this to happen it is not only important that individuals review their daily experiences, but that groups and institutions review their meetings and the quality of their working relationships. Only through a review process of meetings and decisions can we begin to remind each other what we have achieved and not achieved, recall our antisocial nature, and gradually build that loyalty and caring which make mutual development possible.

A second balancing factor to be experienced in new living and working arrangements is a growing individual awareness of our own untransformed sides. Rudolf Steiner refers to this as the "double."[7] Especially in conflict situations we can notice that suddenly we are consumed by anger, or hatred. In others, there may be a cold, manipulative hatred which seeks to inflict pain. Often both qualities are present. In this experience we see the faces of evil, a Luciferic and Ahrimanic presence in our soul. To acknowledge the presence of such qualities as "mine," as requiring transformation and inner development, is to begin to take spiritual beings—including ourselves—seriously.

So far we have concentrated on how human relationships and new working groups can provide balance through making us aware of our antisocial nature, and our untransformed "double." This reflecting, mirror function is an essential service we can do for each other, no matter how badly or semi-consciously. It is something for which we need to learn gratitude, because it is through the wisdom of destiny that we are given those experiences and images which suggest areas for self-transformation.

The mirror function of working groups and of conscious relationships can be seen as a call to see ourselves more clearly and to develop. Fortunately another quality is present when we live and work with each other over time—an invitation to develop interest, understanding, and ultimately the beginning of love. This invitation is subtle and only becomes apparent over time. We may notice that a particular person always brings the discussion back to a point that we left ten minutes ago. At first this is annoying, perhaps even maddening, but then one day we notice the important clarifications that often result. We become interested, we listen to how the person expresses his or her thoughts, how this annoying quality can work positively, as well as negatively. This spark of initial interest is a door through which we can proceed. We may ask what temperament, what background, what life history expresses itself in this person? In short, we seek some understanding of the other. The more we learn the more we appreciate how different people are, how fundamentally other is their experience of the world. This process can lead to friendship and to the thought, "how wonderful that they are different—that there are differences between people." Perhaps some weeks or months later when we are facing an important decision in the group, the same person again brings up an issue left behind long ago, this time negatively so that others react badly. The resulting injury to that person leads us to act. After the meeting we go to the person, we discuss it and share some of our observations, not out of anger, but out of understanding and compassion.

We all have experiences of this kind but perhaps don't realize their fundamental importance. Initially, when we begin to listen we are turning our thought consciousness outward—turning doubt into interest—moving from a closed gesture to an open one. This turning of thought into active listening—into interest—requires effort. It is a willing-thinking listening process. Once accomplished, it often activates our feeling toward the other, transforming our natural sympathies and antipathies into an organ of perception, into a feeling understanding, an objective empathy. In so doing we replace the natural sympathies and antipathies with Christian understanding. This is important in social life, for the butterfly collection in our soul is a kind of coffin for others, making them unfree. To rid ourselves of fixed images of others, to develop a picture based on warm understanding, carrying in it a recognition of their striving spirit—and of that which they are struggling to transform—is a vital social deed to which Steiner repeatedly drew attention.[8]

A warm and objective understanding of another in our feeling life can then also fire the will, transforming egotistic impulses into deeds of compassion and ultimately of love.

The "mirror" and "invitation" functions of working relationships in connection with individual development have now been briefly characterized, and can be summarized in the following manner.

The Mirror   **The Invitation**

Awareness	Doubt		Thinking	Interest		Development
of	Sympathies and Antipathies		Feeling	Understanding		of
Antisocial	Egotism		Willing	Compassion		Social
Forces						Forces
		The Double			The Ego	

As experiences, the mirror and the invitation are not sequential. Sometimes genuine interest in another can make us aware that we have in the past not listened, but have met their thoughts with doubt. Sometimes it is the other way around; the awareness of our antisocial side creates a mood of humility which leads to genuine interest.

In looking at this process it is important to recognize a basic polarity which Steiner describes as the fundamental phenomenon of all social life. In meeting others we are, as it were, oscillating between being awake in ourselves, formulating responses, attending to our feelings—the antisocial forces; and falling asleep into others listening to them and living into their reality—the social forces.[9] This swing between waking to ourselves and sleeping into others is natural and can be observed in every conversation we have. To develop new social forces our ego must be strong enough to maintain consciousness while listening to and understanding others. As in all inner development, this requires a continuous and conscious struggle. A small indication of this struggle is the experience of how tiring it is to truly listen to another person for a period of time—and how enlivening to listen to oneself. I think that the practice of maintaining consciousness while using one's soul faculties of thinking, feeling and willing to understand the other is analogous to maintaining consciousness in sense-free meditation.

This is mainly because in consciously seeing the other we are perceiving the other's ego, his or her spiritual essence and force. It is this ego force which normally lulls us into semi-consciousness and which arouses the antisocial forces in us as a form of self-protection. To develop conscious social qualities is to be able to maintain consciousness in the spiritual presence of the other.[10] This is difficult and requires ego strength. It is also a form of spiritual cognition.

The task of developing conscious social qualities is enormously important for the individual, for others, for the future of social life, and indeed for the earth. For the individual its fundamental importance lies in the fact that such a development occurs only if the individual has assumed some control and mastery in his or her soul. As long as we are thought, felt and willed—pushed like a reed by the turbulence of our soul moods—true interest and understanding of others is not possible. So in becoming aware of our antisocial natures, in gaining glimpses of our "double," and in attempting to develop interest, understanding and compassion for others, we are on the road to attaining mastery in our soul.

Its importance for others, for social relationships, can be experienced daily. Who has not had at least one experience of being truly listened to and felt the warmth, enjoyed the resulting clarity of thought, and experienced the wonder of a true conversation. At still another level, to live and work with others who carry a true picture of ourself is to be continuously encouraged in the struggles of life. Perhaps most importantly, groups of people who are striving to develop conscious social qualities have the possibility of helping to fulfill each other's destiny. The antisocial qualities block a recognition of karmic relationships and possibilities. More conscious social qualities and relationships create a clearing in which karmic perspectives can be seen and worked with.

For groups and institutions seeking to serve the needs of the time, the development of new social faculties is the leaven which makes such service possible. We may talk about creating a vessel for the spirit, but unresolved anger, hidden jealousies and disagreements, and latent conflicts pollute the space between us. To create a soul and spirit space which positive working hierarchies find of interest and in which they can be present requires the jointly created substance of true caring for the spirit and for each other.[11]

There is also a less visible connection between the development of conscious social faculties and the future of social life. In a lecture on the work of the angels in the astral body of the human being, Rudolf Steiner indicates that the angels are weaving three pictures into the unconscious of individuals. These images are: thoughts are real and are capable of penetrating to spiritual realities; meetings between human beings can acquire a sacramental quality when we recognize the divine in each other; and people in the future will not be able to sleep as long as others are suffering.[12] These three images are meant to form the basis of a future society characterized by freedom in cultural life, equality in the political and rights life, and brotherhood in economic life. However, according to Steiner, the healthy working of these images can only come about if people are capable of bringing them to consciousness through their own activity. If this does not happen these images will function destructively.

If we regard these statements from the perspective of developing social qualities, then two connections become apparent. Firstly, the bringing forth of such qualities is a work of transformation which is made possible by the work of the angels in us and is at the same time the very activity which can bring these images to consciousness. Secondly, the qualities of interest, understanding, and compassion in human souls provide the basis for what Rudolf Steiner described as the historical necessity of the threefold social order. We may shy away from the seemingly impossible task of restructuring current society, but I think we dare not shy away from the task of inner development which will make such external restructuring possible in the future.

The work of self-development leading to new social qualities also has significance for the earth. In an early series of lectures Rudolf Steiner portrays the nine hierarchies and the nine counter qualities connected to the inner layers of the earth. For example, he connects the fire earth, the sixth layer, to base drives and obsessions, and the splinterer, the eighth, to conflict, war, violence, and all forms of disharmony.[13] It is a picture strongly reminiscent of the Manichaean worldview of a "Terra Pestifera," a demonic world of darkness and of matter, and the "Terra Lucida," the world of light and goodness.[14] In both Manichaean Christianity and in spiritual science man has the possibility, the task as an earthly and spiritual being, to transform himself out of freedom, and in so doing to transform the earth and the forces of darkness. Soul transformation is a cosmic deed with spiritual and earthly consequences. To make this more understandable, there is a connection between hitting a child out of blind anger and the forces of violence in the earth. As Manes taught, every step toward the world of light in us weakens the world of darkness in us and in the world. It transforms spiritual, psychological, and ultimately physical reality.

I have suggested some of the ways in which working with others can balance the antisocial forces in us and act as a stimulus to the development of conscious social qualities. The importance of such a development process within human souls for the future of social life and of the earth has also been indicated. If we can remember what is at stake, then we can also encourage each other to take steps toward becoming more social and more truly human.

Notes

1. I am in particular referring to two lectures, "Social and Antisocial Instincts," Dec. 6, 1918 contained in R. Steiner, *The Challenge of the Times*, Anthroposophic Press, N.Y. 1941-82 and "Social and Antisocial Forces in the Human Being," December 12, 1918, published, in the *Anthroposophical Review*, Summer 1979 and Winter 1980, Vol. 1, No. 2,3.

2. R. Steiner, "How Can the Psychological Distress of Today be Overcome?" (Wie kann die Seelische Not der Gegenwart Überwunden werden). English translation in Steiner, *Results of Spiritual Investigation*, SteinerBooks, 1971, p. 100.

3. "Social and Antisocial Forces in the Human Being," Anthroposophical Review, Vol. 1, No. 2, p. 13.

4. "Social and Antisocial Forces in the Human Being." *Anthroposophical Review*, Vol. 1, No. 2, pp. 13-14. For a description of the threefold social order see R. Steiner *The Threefold Social Order*, Anthroposophic Press, Spring Valley, N.Y. 1966 and R. Steiner *The Social Future*, A. Press 1945.

5. "How Can the Psychological Distress of Today Be Overcome?" pp. 105-106.

6. Marjorie Spock, *Reflections on Community Building*. Self-published. This excellent essay contains many important insights on human relationships. Available through St. George Bookservice, Spring Valley, N.Y.

7. See *Journal for Anthroposophy*, Number 37, Summer, 1983.

8. "Social and Antisocial Forces in the Human Being. *Anthroposophic Review*, p. 16.

9. "Social and Antisocial Instincts," pp. 123-125.

10. See George van Arnim, "Soul Forces in Human Encounters," *Curative Education and Social Therapy*, No. 4, 1982, for an extensive discussion of the waking and sleeping aspect of human encounter in connection to the ego sense.

11. See Bernard Lievegoed, *Towards the 21st Century: Doing the Good*.

12. R. Steiner, *The Work of the Angels in Man's Astral Body*, Lecture given in Zurich 9 Oct. 1912. Rudolf Steiner Press, London 1972.

13. R. Steiner, *Vor den Tore der Theosophie*, GA 95, Lecture of Sept. 4, 1906, Dornach, Switzerland.

14. See Eugen Roll, *Mani, der Gesandte des Lichts*, T. Ch. Mellinger Verlag. Stuttgart, 1976, pp. 35-56 for a description of Manichaean cosmology. Also Hugo Reimann, *Manichaismus-das Christentum der Freiheit*. Philosophisch-Anthroposophischer Verlag, Dornach 1941-80. In English, Ehrenfried Pfeiffer, Streams in Esoteric Christianity, Spring Valley, N.Y. (St. George Book Service) and A. Steffen, *The Death Experience of Manes, A Drama*, Folder Editions, 1970, N.Y. and Dornach, Switzerland.

Ideas that Destroyed Russia and Ideas that Can Rebuild

Clopper Almon

I. The Consequences of Philosophical Materialism

In 1917, a new government in Russia set out to build a new state, a new economy, and indeed, a new Man. Today, as Russians openly compare their country to one which has lost a war, it is hard but important to recall how this Great Experiment once captured the imagination of idealists throughout the world. Here at last, many of them felt, would be a government based upon a scientific understanding of man and history. That Experiment has clearly led Russia and all the Soviet Union through experiences and into a situation for which no friend could possibly have hoped.

It is tempting but dangerous to blame this failure on the personalities of those who came to power, or to see the roots of its failure in specifically Russian factors. To do so would be to cheat ourselves of its lessons. Rather, I believe, this experiment has written in letters of continental proportions the consequences of the philosophy on which it was based.

That philosophy originates in western European thinking and is still very much alive today. In the West, we have confined it to the intellectual atmosphere of the intelligentsia and have only to a limited degree applied it in practice. In Russia, it was embraced wholeheartedly not only by the leaders but by the rank and file of the working class from which the government drew its support. Recognizing in the present Soviet situation the consequences of this philosophy seriously applied to life makes that situation a vital concern to everyone anywhere in the world, especially in Western Europe and America, the home territory of this philosophy.

This philosophy, of course, is materialism. It begins from our proposition that science has "proven" that matter is primary. "Soul" or "spirit," if they exist at all, are merely some sort of emanations of matter. The origin of life is to be sought in material processes; its evolution is determined by the struggle for material existence of species whose nature and gradual transformation is determined by the material structures of genetic material. Man's whole physiological organization is seen as serving the needs of material life with a single command post in the brain and obedient "levers" in the limbs or heart or lungs. Man's culture consists of his manipulation of matter. His society depends on the relations of material production.

Given that man embodies just one principle—the material one—his society also need embody only one principle. Everything in society, then, derives from material production. Materialistic physiology sees in the brain the central command post for the whole body. In an instinctive analogy with this supposed organizing and commanding role of the brain, material production, and indeed, all of society is organized from the central "command post." The state becomes first and foremost this central controller. Protection of "human rights" is the business of this state only insofar as it is advantageous for it do so to maximize output. Diversity of opinion is tolerated where—and only where—it is useful for material production. Education, science, and culture are sponsored to the extent that they promote material production. The New Man is brought up to love being a lever in the marvelous machine omnisciently designed to maximize his material well-being.

This picture, the beautifully logical idyll implied by materialistic philosophy, fits with surprising accuracy the Brezhnevian Soviet Union which I came to know in the 1970s and early 1980s. It was no proper reproach that it failed to protect what Westerners called "human rights." That was never part of the plan. What rights does matter have? Any man is just matter. When I visited bookstores in Moscow in those days, I felt how barren they were in "soul-searching" writing about public issues, not to mention "soul-feeding" writing about philosophy or religion. This barrenness was all the more depressing in a land renowned for its "soul." Obviously, I had failed to shake off my bourgeois notions and realize that I had no soul to search or feed. Even science became strongly utilitarian. Aside from a few really beautiful mathematical books, science for the "Renaissance man" seemed to be very rare. But what place had the soaring spirit of the Renaissance in the life of a "lever?" No, Soviet society could hardly be faulted for the absence of what it never undertook to provide.

All the more stunning is the ultimate failure of the system to provide even the material well-being to which everything else had been sacrificed. It is not my purpose to analyze in detail how this failure came about, but it was not for lack of adequate centralization of power or obedience of subordinates. The one-principle centralization was carried out with remorseless thoroughness.

The catastrophe of central planning and central political control of the economy, rights, and culture is, in fact, not a Russian failure, though the Russians and the other nationalities in the Soviet Union have borne the brunt of it. It is, rather, the "fruit" of a whole philosophical outlook which has its roots, stem, and leaves in the West. The "truth" of a philosophical system is best judged by its effects on those who follow it. Seen in that way, the Soviet Union has been a testing ground of materialism; and it is materialism—not Russia—which has failed the test. We in the West must look upon the situation in the Soviet Union and say, "There are the consequences of *our* way of *thinking*." We must bear our share of responsibility for what they now suffer.

Clearly, we owe them one. We owe them a philosophical outlook with better consequences for those who take it seriously.

II. A Human-Centered Public Philosophy

Is there a philosophical outlook which, applied to the organization of society, could produce something not only better than what now prevails in the USSR but also better than what prevails in the West? I think there is. Indeed, I would regard it as the ultimate disaster of the Great Experiment if—after all that the people in the USSR have endured—they were now to adopt as a model the economic and social system of any other country. I do somehow believe in a destiny for these people, in a calling to bring to humanity something that can be emulated by all.

Clearly, the West has brought such a gift to humanity. It is democracy. We have also shown a way to high material standards of living, but at a cost in terms of environment, business turmoil, personal failure, psychological strain and emptiness, and most recently, drug addiction—which should give a nation pause before setting out to follow our path.

In point of fact, contemporary Western society lacks a coherent philosophy. To develop one carefully step-by-step far exceeds the bounds of this small essay. But the outlines and main result are clear, simple, and can be understood without elaborate development. Such a philosophy must recognize, I believe, three clear and distinct functions in society. These functions arise from three distinct sets of needs. The functions in society which meet those needs must be as independent of one another as are the needs which they meet. They must cooperate, but one function does not derive its justification for existence from another, nor is it controlled or dominated by another. If I may take an example from my own work, we give three required courses for first-year graduate students in economics: one course in microeconomics, one in macroeconomics, and one in econometrics. All three professors should cooperate and coordinate their teaching. But suppose the professor of macro should say to the other two, "look here, your disciplines exist to support mine, so let me tell you what you must teach and how to do it." You may well imagine that any such attempt to achieve "harmony" would produce exactly its opposite.

What then are the three groups of needs and the corresponding functions? Man has a material body, to be sure, and he has needs arising from that body. Meeting those bodily needs is the business of the economic system or first *function*.

But Man has not only material, bodily needs. He also needs recognition as a being with rights. It is as certain as "death and taxes" that the pursuit of economic activity will lead to conflicts in which rights must be determined and protected. This need arises also in personal conflicts which have little to do with the economy. The function which determines and protects those rights we will call the "political state" or just "state," the second *function*. The need for rights arises because, to use the traditional term, Man has a soul. That is, he has a capacity for thinking, feeling, and willing which in no way derives from the matter of his body but is a separate entity indwelling that body.

Even giving Man rights and economic goods and services will leave him quite discontented if he has no way to feel that he is making a contribution.

This drive to contribute is so strong that it is remarkable that it is usually overlooked. Karl Marx is himself a splendid example of a man with an enormous drive to contribute. One who, as I do, deals constantly with young people in their early twenties realizes, if he is sensitive, that they have a great need to find a way in which, through their work, they can bring something "of themselves" into the world. Everything in society which helps people to unfold their capacities we will designate the third, the "cultural" *function*. It includes education, science, art, and religion. To use the traditional term again, this need to unfold something of ourselves arises because man has a spirit. Thus, the three distinct functions refer to the three components of Man: body, soul, and spirit.

Clearly, if the economic system (or a political state whose primary function is to run the economy) sets about to determine rights, those rights will be determined by the economically strongest. That would clearly be "to set the goats to guard the cabbages." If the rights state undertakes an economic activity, like running a railroad, one can be sure that it is only a matter of time until either the railroad gets enmeshed in bureaucracy designed to protect rights and loses money endlessly, or rights get heedlessly disregarded in the economic interest of the railroad. (Governments are notoriously poor regulators of their own economic enterprises.) If the political rights state undertakes to select "the one best system" for education, one is very likely to soon find the schools in the condition of the "public" schools in the USA, a system as close to catastrophe as the Soviet economy.

Each function needs the other two. But if one attempts to dominate the others, the whole system is soon in trouble. In that simple principle, one finds the crux of the problems of the USSR, the USA, and indeed, of every country I know. One may also have there the way out of many problems.

In particular, the three-function idea is the only workable way to deal with the nationalities question. Nationalities relate to culture, not much to rights, and certainly not to economics, which scorns barriers of language and culture unless they are heavily defended. If it is clear that many cultures can intermingle in the same region, each having its schools and churches, each enjoying full protection of rights and full participation in the economy, then there is little incentive to set up nation states. Indeed, the whole idea of national states begins to seem pretty outmoded.

I should make clear that I am not suggesting any blueprint for organizations. I have deliberately spoken of functions, not organizations. The important point is not the organization but the realization of the importance of the separation of the functions. For example, if one can get to the realization that educational philosophy and methods can be determined only by those directly involved in teaching, and that it is totally inappropriate for the political state to determine in any way—either by legislative act or bureaucratic regulation—how teachers teach, then it would hardly matter if teachers were paid by the state. And if that concept is lacking, no manner of ingenious voucher system for independent schools can work. The most mixed-up system can work well if everyone understands what is to be done and what is inadmissible.

One may say, "Yes, your three-function idea sounds good, but politicians will never give up the control they have on schools or the economy." If there is any lesson to be learned from the events of 1989-1990 in East Europe and the USSR, it is surely that when an idea's time has come, the impossible can happen with blinding speed.

There is a striking relation between the three functions and the "Liberty, Equality, Fraternity" motto of the French Revolution. This relation was noted by Rudolf Steiner, who saw in the three-function idea the hope of Europe after World War I. Steiner saw that "equality" makes sense for the rights state, but no sense at all in culture or economics. (We are certainly not all equal earners, nor do we have equal economic needs. Similarly in the cultural sphere. Are we all equally good pianists?) Likewise, "Liberty" is appropriate for the cultural function—the poet should be allowed to write any poem he likes—but it makes little sense in economic life, which is all about behavior under the constraints of budget and production possibilities.

That leaves "fraternity" to match with the economic function. It is usual to rebel at this thought and say, "That is nonsense. Economics is all about cutthroat competition. It has nothing to do with fraternity." That is true enough of capitalistic mores. But it is also true that efforts to attend to the needs we feel for fraternity through "welfare systems" set up by the political state have proven extremely costly, highly bureaucratic, resented by the beneficiaries, and altogether rather unsatisfactory. But is that the only possibility? Remember that the medieval guilds, composed of the closest economic competitors, provided essential social security for their members. Labor unions to this day often provide some form of social insurance. Even such fierce competitors as economic consultants have been known to look out for one another. But we are a long way from really achieving "fraternity" in the economic system.

The achievement of "fraternity" through the economic system may be the great challenge for the people of the East who have endured seventy years of Communism. Can the suffering of those years be metamorphosed into a new caring for those who cannot care for themselves, a caring that works through the economic system and with the efficiency of that system, that brings joy to those who give and gratitude to those who receive, that somehow lifts up and redeems the economic system? To develop an efficient economy which meets the needs of consumers and producers, yet achieves fraternity in the process, would be an accomplishment comparable to the development of workable democracy. Could that be the great mission and destiny of the Russian soul?

III. An Alternative Form of Industrial Ownership

One of the fundamental questions of the restructuring of the Soviet Union concerns the form of industrial ownership. In the USSR, the present predominant form is state ownership; in the West, it is the joint stock company. Not surprisingly, it is frequently suggested that Soviet firms should be sold off to stockholders. Somehow, it seems to be thought, having private stockowners will quickly make the firms more efficient. In fact, however, such a move would, I believe, bring few advantages, many disadvantages, and would close one of the hopeful routes to a new consciousness in industry.

The supposed advantages of the joint-stock form of ownership are few and illusory. Its primary purpose should be to have ultimate control of the company in the hands of owners who have deeply committed themselves to the long-term success of the firm. In fact, the share owner of a typical publicly listed American firm has little more involvement with it than a bettor on a horse race has with the horse. The private direct investor is rapidly disappearing. In the United States, the holdings of private investors fell by forty percent (some $550 billion dollars) between the end of 1983 and the end of 1989. Meanwhile, institutional investors (pension funds, mutual funds, insurance companies) have poured over twice that sum into the market. It is a very rare institution which makes any positive contribution to the effective management of the firms in which it holds stock. They are mere spectators at the stock market horse race. Most institutions are after only one thing: short-term "performance," that is to say, news which makes the value of the stock go up because of the impression it makes on outsiders who know little about what is really going on in the firm. If the firm fails to produce that sort of news, the institution simply sells. This tendency to "punt" at exactly the crucial moment when the owners should be most actively involved has led The *Economist* to characterize the institutions as "punter capitalists." (May 5, 1990)

The second purpose of the stock—to attract capital for highly risky but potentially very profitable ventures—has now been largely taken over by the "junk" bond market.

On the other side, the problems with the joint-stock form of ownership are many. One of the most evident is the scope that it gives for hostile takeovers. The management of a firm which is doing well enough may suddenly find itself on the verge of being displaced by the management of another firm which has offered to buy its stock from stockowners who have no particular connection with the firm. Consequently, prudent managers spend a considerable effort guarding against such takeovers.

Worse, when a firm has come into some difficulty which has caused the value of its stock to drop more than it really should have, the management faces the double problem of overcoming the original difficulty and fighting off the attacks of hostile raiders. The legal fees and management time devoted to such defenses can be major costs.

The best defense is often to keep up the price of the stock. Since public stockowners generally have very little inside information on how the company is being run, they are very much influenced by profits and dividends. In any well-managed company, there arc many costs which are really investments—costs for research and development, advertising, employee education and welfare, and customer service. Any manager, no matter how incompetent, can briefly increase the profits and dividends of such a firm by cutting back on these expenses. He will be rewarded for doing so by seeing the price of the stock rise and perhaps by the offer of the presidency of another firm, where he can play the same nefarious trick and leave the first firm to its fate. Thus, the joint-stock form of ownership leads to the sort of myopia which is becoming more and more characteristic of American industry.

Within the firm, the joint-stock form of ownership has no good effects. The fundamental fact in such a firm is that the earnings of the firm ultimately belong to the stockholder. Workers need to be motivated. It is well-known that appealing to them to make the stockholders rich is the poorest form of motivation. Yet, disguise it how you may, the "bottom line" in a stock company is to enrich the stockholders. The stockowners are the residual beneficiaries of the efforts of the employees of the company. Yet it is impossible for the employees to feel any loyalty to these stockowners, for they cannot usually know who they are and, even if they knew today, there would be others tomorrow, whose loyalty to the company lasts only until they see some blip in the stock price or hear some hot tip. Likewise, the stockowners feel no human connection to the employees, customers, or suppliers of the company. This situation does not lead to efficiency, but to mistrust. Various contracts designed to deal with the mistrust actually reduce the efficiency of the firm.

The strongest point of the joint-stock firm has been its ability to raise funds for risky endeavors. The recent development of the junk bond market, however, has shown that investors are willing to put money into high-risk ventures without having ownership and control over those ventures and without having unlimited profits in case of success. Even this strongest point is not a property unique to stocks.

There is an alternative very simple form of ownership—the non-stock corporation. There are countless examples in the United States. They run schools, universities, hospitals, churches, research institutions, and some industrial and commercial firms. These organizations are often run with efficiency not exceeded in stock companies. They are not afflicted with the myopia or with the defenses against takeovers endemic among stock companies.

One very interesting example of such a company is Townsend and Bottom. Before the current collapse of construction of electric power plants, it was the largest constructor of coal-fired plants in the United States. It was a family held firm, but the president, C.E. Bottom realized that should he retire and sell some of his stock, the firm would be an attractive target for takeover by other firms interested mainly in closing it to reduce competition in the area. Mr. Bottom was also very sensitive to the interpersonal relations between himself as president, and largest stockowner of the company, and the other employees. He wanted a relationship in which it would be clearer that his management was aimed at the welfare of the company, not solely his own profit.

He found the innovative solution of creating a non-stock company whose bonds were exchanged for the common stock of the previous company. The new company has a self-perpetuating board of directors. This move completely solved the problem of hostile takeovers. It also subtly changed the relations within the firm. The firm operated quite profitably under the new organization for several years until the whole electrical construction industry collapsed. Curiously, it was then the ability of the new organization to arrange a friendly merger without a stock transfer with another company which then held the key to a way out of the difficulties which had put out of business all of the other independent companies in that line of work.

This example shows that the non-stock corporation can manage and arrange financing every bit as effectively as stock corporations. Further, it avoids the pressure to make myopic decisions and offers the possibility of intra-firm industrial relations based on trust and mutual interest rather than antagonism. It is a form to which the Soviet state-owned industries could easily migrate and through which they might then achieve the fraternity in the economic sphere which has so far eluded the Western countries.

Obviously, this form of ownership alone will not solve all the problems of the Soviet Union, but it might help avoid a new host of problems that stock companies bring. The fundamental idea, of course, is to separate the economic life from the state so that the state can take care of rights and the economy can achieve efficient satisfaction of material wants. The best place to begin that withdrawal of the state from the economy is, I believe, to remove the legal ban on buying and selling the ruble. With one stroke, the ruble then becomes convertible; and all the distorted price system and the bureaucracy that exists by means of it would be swept away in days. This would be radical surgery, but it will be quick, and the recovery would be quick. The country could then get to work on solving its real problems instead of toying with those created artificially. In the new milieu then created, the private non-stock company can play a creative role.

From Consumer to Producer in the Spiritual Sphere

Herbert Witzenmann

When we regard the situation of today, we see that it comes to meet us with a particular demand. Concerning this particular demand, the historian Toynbee has made a significant statement in a recently published essay. He points out that one of the most character-istic and serious symptoms of the present is the increase in violence in all areas of the earth and that, alongside this symptom of the increase in violence, there exists yet another symptom, the increase in pitilessness, which is evidenced among other things in the fact that nowadays there is no longer any underprivileged class of society, but that in all classes and levels of the populace there are underprivileged people, that is to say the old, the weak, such people who are not provided for by large-scale organizations. These two symptoms of violence and lovelessness are drawing humanity into a constantly worsening state of brutality. Toynbee states that every government is really based on force and that no improvement can be expected as long as nations do not discard the two principles of force and pitilessness. In response to such an utterance, we can feel the challenge of the times appealing to our own hearts, to find a style of working which can confront this violence and pitilessness with a positive example: the working together of free individualities. Certainly, Rudolf Steiner has said that people will and must become more and more individualized and differentiated, that this will and must bring about an increasingly greater danger of estrangement, that there will be no guarantee of safety in the future—this future has in the mean-time become the present—and that there will only be one remedy, to live with trust in the spiritual world which expresses itself in single human beings as the impulses of the individual.

Now, to these symptoms which I have mentioned with reference to Toynbee, I should like to add a third which is significant and characteristic for everyone, but particularly, I think, for young people, and that is, the wish to escape from being a consumer and being part of a society consisting of consumers. This dissatisfaction, this wanting to escape from a society of consumers with its forced production and its surplus of goods, is one of the deepest impulses of our time, especially in young people. Here we encounter a situation similar to the one which confronted Rudolf Steiner at the end of the first World War with regard to the proletariat. The proletariat at that time wanted to escape from a society based on property and commercial interests and it possessed tremendous forces, impulses of will, to do so, but it only had the old manner of thinking and habits of feeling. It wanted to escape from this old situation with old forces. That was the tragedy at that time. And the whole of present-day humanity is in a similar situation. The whole of humanity has actually become the proletariat. Fundamentally, everyone wants in his innermost being—even those who are at home in this society of consumers—to escape from it, particularly young people. But they do not yet know how to do so, and consequently they slip back again and again into the old habits of thinking and feeling, into the very attitudes which brought about this consumer situation. So that progress can only be made when people learn to overcome the consumer situation in themselves and instead of being consumers, become producers in the sense of Rudolf Steiner's words: "My whole work is only the apparatus on which one learns gymnastics." The consumption of this work has no value.

If one wants to help, and particularly to help young people, the first thing is not necessarily to provide answers—of course, one must also in a tactful way provide answers, as far as one can—but it is much more important to try to lead people to the point where they create the prerequisites in themselves, whereby they can answer their own questions, and provide their own counsel. Wilhelm von Humboldt said that if you really want to counsel someone you should not give him advice. If young people are to help themselves through an inner exertion of will, through inner discipline and exercise, then it is just the overcoming of the consumer mentality which is urgent. In this sense, I should like to attempt a brief contribution. I should like to take as my starting point something which one often meets as a question particularly from young people. This is the question concerning the path of inner training, of meditation. I intentionally choose the most delicate question just because it cannot receive a direct answer, since the best and most productive course is not to speak of the results and experiences of meditation if one wishes to make progress in one's meditative life. Nevertheless, in the preparatory stage leading to meditation one can make significant observations. I should like to present observations of this kind as they might emerge in a living way during the course of a conversation, observations which need in no way be adopted by others, but which may serve as a stimulus to develop out of oneself whatever corresponds to one's own nature.

Let us consider the seed meditation which you all know. Not only can it be meditated, it allows one to observe the preparatory stage of consciousness—that which precedes supersensible impressions or presentiments—with the sober, reflective calmness of the scientist.

Out of a seed, we can let the plant appear before us in an inner formative process in somewhat the same wonderful way in which it occurs in Goethe's elegiac lines on metamorphosis. Then we see rising before this inner, active process a growing, a striving from the darkness of the earth into light, from the formless to the formed, from the colorless to the colorful, from the arid into the juicy. We follow these metamorphoses of plant growth, their expansions and contractions, closing to complete the ring of growing and becoming, which in turn becomes a link in the chain of life. But if at the same time we fix our observant gaze on ourselves, we notice that this meditation can only succeed if we produce a stronger power of will than we do in ordinary life. In ordinary life, our will is actually drawn along by that to which we are accustomed, by outer influences and coercions. It actually submerges itself in our activity and therefore eludes our consciousness. When we meditate, however, we must make a free decision to activate our will. And it is through this effort that we become conscious of it.

But it enters our consciousness in a strange way. Under ordinary conditions, it is always directed outward. Now it is directed inward. A complete reversal of the will occurs. And now as a consequence, the following experience can perhaps make itself delicately felt. This reversal of the will which is directed inward on the seed or on any other phenomenon or being of the world, is like sending down roots into the essential nature of things. From these roots of will, the trunk of our own being begins to grow up.

We notice, when we continue this self-observation, that our life of feeling also undergoes a transformation. We feel ourselves wondrously refreshed through living like this in the growth of a plant. Green shoots begin to sprout in us, and perhaps even to blossom, and we notice that, in this sprouting and blossoming, we overcome the consumer attitude, the consumer mentality. No longer do we consume the seed, as we not only do by chewing it with our jaws, but which we also consume by simply accepting it, or simply accepting any other object of knowledge in order to nourish our soul-life with it. But now within the "greening" in our soul, in our feeling life, the seed begins to unfold its leaves all over again. It achieves, so to speak, a new dimension to grow in. Not only does our relationship to the world change in that we provide the beings which are part of it with a new opportunity of growth, rather than consuming them, no, also our relationship to ourselves changes, as I have already touched on, for we begin ourselves to spring up and grow out of the elements and the beings of which the world is composed.

But this springing growth is evinced in the sphere of our feeling life by still another change of direction. Previously, we reversed the will from an outward to an inward going. In ordinary life our feelings are turned inward and are tremendously interested in themselves. In meditation, our life of feeling turns outward. We feel ourselves inside the being and becoming of things. And this allows another delicate experience to present itself. Attached to the trunk which is growing from the roots of the will, now, suddenly, wings appear, wings of feeling, for in the spiritual sphere roots and hovering do not contradict each other, just as Pherecydes, the European forebear of us all, imagined the world as a winged oak. This feeling life which is no longer confined to its own narrow limits and, in its limitation, is estranged from the world, now lives at one with the world and gives us the wings which support us in the world.

Thirdly, something changes in the life and events of our cognitional faculty. The processes which underlie our cognitional life, our representational faculty, usually elude our observation. Only in exceptional circumstances do they enter into our consciousness in a living way. Usually we only have the dead final products of these processes of our cognitional life in our consciousness. This means that we move in a bloodless world of shadows. But when, in meditation, we send down the roots of the will into things and spread the wings of feeling, we experience the law of plant growth, of the formative force, which lives both in us and in things themselves.

In this way, our cognitional life is now two-sided, like a Janus head, its gaze turned both in an inward and an outward direction. And now on this winged trunk with its roots sent down by the will, blossoms begin to appear, the blossoms of cognitional knowledge. The blossom, too, has two aspects towards which it turns. With its perfume, its radiant beauty of color, the blossom turns outward, inwardly it conceals the seed.

If we now ask ourselves: What has actually taken place, what are the forces through which our own being is conjured up once more out of the being of things as something that takes root and blossoms and has pinions? How does this seed ripen in our meditative experience? Then we must answer: It ripens, it grows, not through the force of nature, but through a force which lies in our own being. And when, now, to conclude, we inquire as to the nature of this force, we can say: It is a force which counteracts the forces of death that are also at work in our being. These death forces are just the opposite of the process I have been describing. They lead us away from the world, let us become estranged from the world, constrict our feeling life within the narrow limits of what is subjective and egoistic, and finally destroy our physical form. These forces, however, which allow us to sprout roots and blossoms and pinions, they build up our spiritual form, they widen our feeling life beyond its narrow limits out to the periphery, into the encircling horizon, and they unite us finally with the being of the world. They are not the forces of death, but Easter forces of resurrection. And it is these forces of resurrection which spread and move the wings of this blossom- and root-sprouting sapling, in that we ourselves allow our own being to spring up and grow out of the beings of the world. These forces carry our being through incarnations and through the progressive development of consciousness.

Perhaps this may serve as a stimulus to overcome the attitude of the consumer in favor of an inner state of productive soul alertness.

The Biodynamic Movement in Our Time

Herbert Koepf

From the *Journal for Anthroposophy*, Spring 1966, Number 3

It is now almost forty-two years since the biodynamic work in farming and gardening began to unfold. It started with a series of eight lectures given by Dr. Rudolf Steiner at Koberwitz in Silesia at the request of practical farmers and gardeners. In March, 1965, we commemorated the day when, forty years earlier, the founder of modern Spiritual Science left the physical plane. The agricultural movement, which received the name "Biodynamics" soon after it was started, is one of the last of the many cultural impulses originated by Dr. Steiner to come into existence. Having the task of developing and fostering improved methods in farming and gardening, the biodynamic movement finds its job in a very practical field of human life. Its value in our economic and cultural system is therefore to be measured by the practical answers it can give to concrete questions. But to be truly practical, these answers must, in the long run, be based on genuine biological concepts called forth by the ideas of Spiritual Science. Farming, which has already suffered much under the impact of one-sided, non-biological concepts, needs a change of approach.

At the time, when the biodynamic method was started many more farms than there are today were still fairly complete biological unities raising a variety of crops and animal stock and providing self-contained feed-fertilizer circuits of living substances. Fertilizer programs and also pest and weed control were still, to a great extent, based on traditional techniques. Only a relatively few of the many processes and chemicals now employed in refining, fortifying, conditioning, processing and preserving food were known. Help was provided at a time when the powerful impact of modern chemistry and technology on food production was not yet fully effective. The engine which drove things to become what they are today gained great strength during the past thirty to fifty years. This is what we intend to discuss briefly here.

If we ask a farmer what his grievances are, he is likely to speak about economic problems rather than biological ones. It is economic factors which largely control farm management. In this country, about 1/5 of the farmer's net income is government support. When compared with the figure of 100 in 1949, the price index for farm products in 1962 was 79. That part of the population which will find its livelihood in farm work is expected to be reduced to half of its present number by 1980. One man using machines plows more acres than ever before, feeds more animals and transports an increased amount of tonnage of products and supply materials. This trend will continue. Too little time is left to the farmer for patiently watching the living beings he works with. He does not have enough time to let his decisions gradually ripen. It is largely economic pressures which make farmers change into managers of chicken, corn, tobacco or cattle industries. Anticipating, as it were, a situation which was only then beginning to arise, Rudolf Steiner, in the very first lecture of the Agriculture Course, spoke briefly about the fact that the true economic principles of agriculture need to be discovered if farming is to thrive. "No one can judge agriculture who does not derive his judgment from field and forest and the breeding of cattle. All talk of economics which is not derived from the job itself should really cease." This calls for organizing farm work according to the inherent laws of the farm organism itself.

In our modern agriculture, economic factors are increasingly put ahead of biological ones. In the thirties it was soil erosion resulting from over-cropping for quick cash returns, which called for a change in the common malpractices. After the second World War, farmers and gardeners in this country were flooded with an increasing stream of chemicals for fertilizing and for weed and pest control. This trend, which will continue, was described in detail by C. J. Pratt in the June 1965 issue of *Scientific American*. This is what he has to say about the economic aspects of fertilizers: "Of all the short-range factors capable of increasing agricultural production readily—factors including pesticides, improved plant varieties and mechanization—the largest yields and the most substantial returns on invested capital come from chemical fertilizers." We do not analyze this statement as to what is true or false. But we envision here one of the basic forces which fashion farming in our days and will continue doing so for some time in the future.

The biodynamic farmer wants to organize his farm according to the need for conservation and what the life conditions of plants and animals are. In this endeavor, many innovations, for instance new machines, building designs, and plant varieties of modern farming prove to be helpful to him. But there are also conditions which work against what he actually wants to do. How can he cope with the economic pressure we spoke about? There is an answer, based on the history of the biodynamic movement. Biodynamic farms and commercial and home gardens are concentrated mainly in Western and Northwestern Europe and the North American continent. There the movement spread from its beginning. In some countries, a remarkable line of biodynamically grown products are now offered to those interested in getting them. This biodynamic movement, although only recently beginning to gain the respect of official science, also stimulated research in organic farm management, the search for biological disease and pest control and interest in real quality of food production. Although biodynamic farms and gardens are scattered in other parts of the world too, most of them are located in those areas where food production has undergone the most drastic changes as a result of modern technical and chemical practices. In other words, B.D. farms are to be found where the negative side effects of modern farming systems are strongest. However, this should not be considered the main factor which influenced the occurrence of B.D. farms. It is rather the fact that both of the modern systems (technological and biodynamic) call for skilled people with good vocational training. It is true that many turned to Biodynamics because they still had some traditional feeling for the value of the method. But this only helped them to get interested. To continue, requires professionalism. Now, after 40 years' work done by biodynamic farmers in countries with highly developed farm systems, it can be stated that well-operated farms have done and still do well with this method. But its success thus far has been based on the skill and idealism of the individual gardener or farmer. If the movement is to spread to any great degree, more is required. *One will have to find new approaches to organizing the relation between producer and consumer in a way that suits them both.* Little has been achieved thus far in this respect. Much more is needed in such a basic application of the economic principles of agriculture.

Let us now turn to a few examples of biodynamic concepts and see how they compare with those commonly accepted. In the fourth of his agricultural lectures, Rudolf Steiner speaks about fertilizing the soil. "For many plants there is absolutely no hard and fast line between the life within the plant and the life of the surrounding soil in which it is living. … To manure the earth is to make it alive, so that the plant may not be brought into a dead earth and find it difficult, out of its own vitality, to achieve all that is necessary up to the fruiting process. The plant will achieve more easily what is necessary for the fruiting process if it is immersed from the outset in an element of life. Fundamentally, all plant growth has this slightly parasitic quality. It grows like a parasite out of the living earth. And it must be so."

When the plant builds its body, using solid, liquid and gaseous substances given by earth, water and air, these substances are brought to a higher level of organization than they held while outside the plant. They become part of a living system. This system, however, is open to the influence of its environment. Fertilizing the soil must be more than just adding a few inorganic elements. It actually means that the substance which surrounds the roots must be enlivened. A well-ripened compost is organized substance. It does not contain elements in excess; rather, they are present in almost optimum proportions. It contains food for the soil life and growth regulating factors. It has a crumbly and sponge-like consistency from having been chewed and digested by myriads of primitive animals. Gardeners appreciate a compost with this structure. It contains the biodynamic preparations as organizing factors, etc. When it is added to the ground, it will not only furnish nutrients but also stimulate a multitude of bio-chemical, chemical and even physical processes needed to create optimum conditions for the roots of the growing plant.

One may ask: "What is wrong with chemical fertilizers? After all, they increase the yields." The answer is that, using these materials is, in too many cases, a one-sided measure. It may be worthwhile discussing this matter briefly. Thanks to the progress of chemistry, one has learned about the elements of which plants consist. It soon became clear that some of them, like phosphorus, potash, etc. are furnished by the soil. Why not add such elements to the ground instead of depleting it?

Applications of some of these chemical substances increased the yields considerably. A new concept, that of arbitrarily manipulating organisms was born; one determines what their building bricks are and uses one or more of these bricks to manipulate the living whole. Even today relatively few people realize that this is a double-edged concept. However successful it may appear in the beginning, it is non-biological in its essence. It was still a primitive approach when only a few so-called major nutrients were used as fertilizers. As time went on, the list of those needed grew longer. What one did in the beginning was successful because Nature herself took care of the remainder which had not been taken care of by man. But side effects showed up. Such side effects are impaired growth and *decreased* nutritional value of plants, a declining capacity of the soil to properly transfer these fertilizers to the plant, increased susceptibility of plants to pests, diseases, etc.

To avoid bad side effects, fertilizing, above all, must enhance and strengthen the life-functions of the soil, which will then regulate and balance the nutrient supply.

During the last few years, the Biochemical Research Laboratory, together with others, has worked mainly on improved methods of soil fertilizing. Thanks to the work done for a number of years by Mr. Michael Scully in the Midwest, a working and economically feasible system of farm composting has been worked out which meets the special requirements in that area. At another place, an improved compost mixture is now in production which is good with respect to the quality of the compost, the nutrient formula and its fitness for modern farm machinery. Current research deals with the physiological effect on plants or herbs used for the biodynamic preparations and of organic fertilizers and substances which occur in the stubble and roots left in the field after harvesting. It should be emphasized, however, that this country is badly in need of many more large-scale research programs to check on the present gigantic waste of organic fertilizers and the mining of natural soil productivity than our small group can dream of accomplishing at this time. There is a definite need to rebuild the circuits of living substances in Nature which have been destroyed in many places by so-called modern systems of growing food.

Photo © Copyright, Seven Stars Farm

The questionable scheme of manipulating living organisms, to which we have referred, can be found in many metamorphoses. Here are a few examples. The present corn root-worm calamity in the Midwest could be adequately checked if one would quit growing corn continuously. Confining large numbers of animals in mechanized feeding outfits entails sanitation and disposal problems. The Winter 1965 issue of *Biodynamics* gives detailed examples of bad side effects of one particular compound, nitrate. Many other effects of life-manipulation could be cited. Again and again one finds Goethe's words confirmed: "Nothing happens in living Nature that is not in relation to the whole." These words find practical application in biodynamic farming and gardening, which is based on an insight into the mutual relations of soil, plants and animals. It is one of the tasks of our biodynamic work to correct one-sided approaches. What we mentioned about soil fertilization, is only one example in this respect. But the significance of the impulse inaugurated over forty years ago can be clearly recognized today.

Choosing America as a Place for Incarnation or Immigration in the 20th century

Virginia Sease

(Summary of a lecture given at the New York City Branch of the Anthroposophical Society in America on February 13, 1999)

Each person who finds a relation to Anthroposophy treads a unique path of study and meditation that fits his or her specific life situation. Besides this more individual aspect, however, there are general themes that are timeless in their nature and yet sometimes demand attention at a specific moment out of inner historical necessity. As we enter the next century, and thereby the next millennium, such a theme, in my estimation, centers on the relation of the human being to the spiritual hierarchies. This acquires special importance for America due to the unique situation of its folk-spirit.

Whereas other countries such as Italy, Norway, and France have a guiding folk-spirit that is at the level of an Archangel, America does not have an archangelic being as its folk-spirit. America has a being that is higher in rank, an Archai-Being, but this Archai-Being has remained behind in the normal course of evolution. This is in the sense of service, not as a failure, as when certain hierarchical beings do not progress normally and thus stay at a lower degree.

The Archai-beings are also designated by Rudolf Steiner as the Spirits of Personality. From an external perspective, especially if one has immigrated to America, the qualities of personality appear much stronger here than in other places in the world. One often hears the phrase: "In America *every*body is *some*body," and for those who have immigrated to America even in childhood, the great test often seems to be how to become "somebody." How can one activate one's personality, which is not even the earthly ego, in order to project a countenance? Otherwise, a nagging fear creeps in that one will get "lost in the shuffle," unknown and invisible. Even when a person says "I" it serves only to differentiate himself/herself from the rest of the world. Exactly this may give the impression of extreme superficiality in America.

The eternal ego, the essential entelechy, is not encapsulated within the earthly ego. Rudolf Steiner spoke about the relation of the "earthly I" to the "eternal I" in London on the occasion of the founding of the Anthroposophical Society in Great Britain. As one delves into Anthroposophy, one can acquire the feeling that Rudolf Steiner often brought certain insights in specific places. He knew that there were people there who could take up the insights in a comprehensive manner and allow them to find a footing in their souls.

> I gaze into the darkness.
> In it there arises Light –
> Living Light.
> Who is this Light in the darkness?
> It is I myself in my reality.
> This reality of the I
> Enters not into my earthly life;
> I am but a picture of it.
> But I shall find it again
> When with good will for the Spirit
> I shall have passed through the Gate of Death.[1]

So this is the picture of the eternal I. Our own Angel-being helps to mediate between the eternal I and the earthly I of the human being. Thus we speak of our Guardian Angel bringing intuitions, impulses for deeds, warnings.

Another question presents itself today for many people all over the world: What is the relation of the eternal I of the human being to the Christ? At the conclusion of *An Outline of Esoteric Science* the Greater Guardian of the Threshold is revealed to the esoteric pupil as the Christ Being. And in a meditation given to an esoteric pupil at Easter in 1924 Rudolf Steiner addresses this relation:

In the Evening after the Review of the day:

From Grace
May there stream to me Wisdom
May Wisdom bring forth Love for me
May love take part in Grace
May Love create Beauty for me
May Beauty bring me Grace.
(Peace of Soul)

In the Morning: A star above one's head, Christ speaks from the star

Let your soul
Be carried
By my strong force
I am with you
I am in you
I am for you
I am your I.
(Peace of Soul)[2]

(Transl. V.S.)

When the human being says "I" to differentiate himself/herself from other beings, the I is directed outwards. When, however, a person strives to experience the I and turns inward, then from the soul-spiritual sphere this brings one into connection—whether consciously or not—with the spiritual hierarchies. This explains why, for example, one can feel such an inward identification with one's country. Also, we can see why, along the path of self-knowledge, we can come to the question: which spiritual beings are especially active in America, and what is their nature?

It is important to remember that, wherever an individuality incarnates on Earth, whether he/she is born in that location or moves there, two factors play an important role. One factor concerns the etheric geography of that location; the second factor is centered upon the mystery of the Double.

Concerning the first, Rudolf Steiner inaugurated an etheric geography that Günther Wachsmuth[3] then developed further in his early writings. He differentiated four types of ether: warmth ether, light ether, sound or chemical ether, and life ether. These are parallel to the conditions of physical warmth, air, fluid, and solid earth.

Even though the ether qualities are mixed at any given place, generally one specific ether-type predominates according to the geographic location. Following the indications of Günther Wachsmuth, if we take the Atlantic Ocean as a point of departure, from the East Coast of North America to the British Isles and then over to the middle of Europe the sound ether connected with fluidity predominates. Tradition maintains that the sound ether meets the light ether, the airy element, approximately in the area of Vienna. The light ether then extends eastward over to about the Ural Mountains in Russia, where it encounters the warmth or fire ether. The warmth ether projects from the eastern Part of Russia across the Pacific Ocean, over the Hawaiian Islands to the West Coast of North America and on to the Rocky Mountains. From there eastward to the Atlantic, the major portion of North America is under the life ether, the earth element.

In view of the life-ether predominance over such a large area of North America, it seems important to consider how Rudolf Steiner described this ether in another context. In lectures in Torquay, England in 1924, he mentioned the special task of the vital radiation, the vital ray. "These life radiations are the rays which now must enter into our age as something beneficial; because with all of the impulses which should be given in the Michael Age, the connection with the mastery of the life radiation, the vital radiation, should gradually occur. Mainly one must learn not to work in a lifeless, dead way with that which comes from the spiritual, but directly in a living manner. To find living ideas, living concepts, living viewpoints, living feelings, not dead theories, that is the task of this Age."[4] *(Transl. V.S.)*

As this task of the Michael Age is connected with the vital radiation, we may explore its relevance for America and for a person either born in America or who has immigrated to America. A characteristic of America may be summed up as openness. It is open for all kinds of strange phenomena, but it has also always been open to regard seriously the spirit as a reality. We may recall the story connected with the signing of the Declaration of Independence. It was a hot, humid day in Philadelphia, and the deliberations had extended over many hours. Finally, Benjamin Franklin spoke in a vociferous manner that they had all had so many thoughts about what they should do, but had they ever thought to ask the "Lord of Light" how they could proceed more fruitfully? In America it is especially possible to allow the fruits of working out of a spiritual impulse to become visible, to take on physical form.

With regard to the second factor, every person has a so-called geographic Double (not just Americans!). We are not considering now the astral Double, which sometimes has been described flippantly as the leftover baggage from previous incarnations that must be dealt with. Rudolf Steiner describes the geographic Double[5] as an Ahrimanic being who enters into the human being just before the moment of birth and remains with him until just before death. It is important that the Double does not go through death with the human being, which would affect his post-mortem situation. The Mystery of Golgotha prevented the Double from ever gaining enough strength to cross the threshold of death because as the blood of the Christ Being flowed into the earth, the very substance of the earth was changed. The earth itself is, however, the attraction for the geographic Double. In accordance with the earth configuration and its etheric components, the Double chooses, as it were, the human being with whom it wishes to dwell. The human being has nothing to say about this choice!

The Double works through the human will forces, which have a natural connection to the earth, and through the forces of intellect. Whereas these beings possess a tremendously strong will and an incredibly sharp intellect, they cannot gain access to human beings in the realm of feelings. The "beat of heart and lungs," as the Foundation Stone Mantram[6] expresses the middle sphere of the human being, is excluded from the influence of the Double. Thus, the Double accompanies us throughout out earthly life and takes hold of as much of our will and our thinking as we have not been able to permeate with our ego forces.

We can see an underlying connection between the geographic Double which thrives especially well when, as on this continent, the mountains run in a north-south direction in relation to the electromagnetic pole and the life ether, which is connected to the earth element. We can think of the mighty Rocky Mountains in the West and the Appalachian chain in the East. Furthermore, in addition to the geographic Double we must reckon with two other powerful polar opposite beings: Ahriman and Lucifer. The former tries to approach the human being from the future, stimulating a hardening into a programmed form, while the latter, enters from the past and promotes complete license, often a lack of commitment, dissolution of form, and yet also encourages the artistic predisposition. How can a person in America, whether born or transplanted here, keep the essential aspect of his life configuration in place? He is challenged to exercise the regulatory effect of his ego as it permeates his thinking, feeling, and will nature.

Because of the life-ether predominance on this continent it can be especially helpful to turn to the Spirits of Wisdom, or *Kyriotetes*, through whose sacrifice in the distant past of Earth's evolution the life body of the human being was formed. These beings relate especially to the rhythmic system of the human being, which is excluded from the strong influence of the geographic Double.

The Holy Rishis of the ancient Indian epoch experienced the many beings of the Kyriotetes Order of the Sun as a unity. They called that unity *Vishvakarman*. Later, in the ancient Persian epoch, Zarathustra experienced this Kyriotetes realm in the Sun as *Ahura Mazdao*, which was really like a window to see the Christ, the Being of the Sun. Through the Kyriotetes the world ether streams to the earth. That is their great task.

How can we become more aware of what we might call the "countenance" of the Kyriotetes? It is not easy to come from pictures or abstract ideas into a possibility of reading their signature. To read the signature of each hierarchy represents a future task for humankind. For the Kyriotetes it is helpful to study the gesture and physiognomy of the plant world, as the group-souls of the plants live in the Kyriotetes sphere.[7] Another way is to work with the metamorphic qualities of eurythmy forms. Whether one does eurythmy actively, watches a performance, or internalizes the drawings of the eurythmy forms which Rudolf Steiner created, one can enter into an inwardly mobile situation that brings the signature of the Kyriotetes closer.

We have enhanced possibilities during the Michael Age, as Michael is the Intelligence or Regent of the Sun, whose regency will last approximately 300 more years. During this time, "in a definitive form the cosmic forces of the Sun will pass over into the physical body and the etheric body of the human being."[8] This enhances the effectiveness of the task of the Kryiotetes. The etheric body has great possibilities for freedom when it is not totally involved in growth processes, reproduction processes, and so on. The free part of the etheric body can work with ideas, with ideals, and with memory. Within this free part the forces of the Sun can become active. This provides then greater access to the cosmic etheric world where, in certain situations, the Christ being may also be perceived.

Bearing these various considerations in mind, we realize that in a place like America, which has strong geographic Double forces on the one side and the enhanced life-ether relationship to the Kyriotetes on the other, the free middle region of the human being, which comes to expression in the "beat of heart and lungs," gains ultimate significance. Rudolf Steiner gave a meditation for America, which many people have lived with for decades. Its dimensions encompass the dangers of superficial personality traits that prevent feelings from penetrating really deeply into the heart sphere, and also draw attention to the hierarchical beings that support every earnest striving.

> May our feeling penetrate
> Into the center of our heart
> And seek, in love, to unite itself
> With the human beings seeking
> The same goal,
> With the spirit beings who,
> Bearing grace,
> Strengthening us from realms of light
> And illuminating our love
> Are gazing down upon
> Our earnest heartfelt striving.

Notes

1. Given in London on the evening of September 2, 1923. The lecture leading up to this meditative verse is published under the title: "Man as Picture of the Living Spirit." The meditation is quoted in *Verses and Meditations*, Rudolf Steiner Press, 1993.

2. Permission for translation kindly given by the Rudolf Steiner Verlag, Dornach, Switzerland. See Rudolf Steiner, *Collected Works*, GA267, Dornach, 1998.

3. See Guenther Wachsmuth, *Die Aetherische Welt in Wissenschaft, Kunst und Religion*, Vol. 2, Dornach, 1927.

4. See Rudolf Steiner, August 18, 1924, in Torquay, in *True and False Paths in Spiritual Investigation*, Rudolf Steiner Press, 1985.

5. See Rudolf Steiner, Lecture of November 16, 1917 in St. Gallen, *Geographic Medicine*, Mercury Press, New York, 1986.

6. See Rudolf Steiner, *The Christmas Conference for the Foundation of the General Anthroposophical Society*, 1923-24, Anthroposophic Press, 1990.

7. See Rudolf Steiner, lecture of April 14, 1912 in *The Spiritual Beings in the Heavenly Bodies and in the Kingdoms of Nature*, Anthroposophic Press, 1992.

8. See Note 4, lecture of August 21, 1924.

Contributors

Georg Kühlewind (1924-2006), a Hungarian philosopher, was a prolific author who lectured widely. Volumes that have been translated into English include *Becoming Aware of the Logos; From Normal to Healthy; and Stages of Consciousness: Meditations on the Boundaries of the Soul.*

Adeline Bianchi taught in public schools for sixteen years and served for nine years on the Western Regional Council of the Anthroposophical Society in America.

Diether Rudloff is an art historian and author. He is the author, among other books, of *Freiheit und Liebe: Gründlagen einer Ästhetik der Zukunft.*

Rex Raab (1914-2004) was a practicing architect in England, Germany, and Switzerland, responsible for the designs of many Waldorf schools, kindergartens, and health clinics. He also designed churches, including the much-praised Neue Kirche of the Movement for Religious Renewal in Berlin.

Cornelius Pietzner is a member of the Executive Council of the world-wide Anthroposophical Society in Dornach, Switzerland. He was formerly director of the Camphill Association of North America and a co-worker at Camphill Soltane.

Christopher Schaefer is Director of the Waldorf School Administration and Community Development Program at Sunbridge College. He is co-author of *Vision in Action: Working with Soul and Spirit in Small Organizations.* He travels extensively as a consultant to businesses, communities, and non-profit organizations.

Clopper Almon is Professor of Economics at the University of Maryland. He is one of the founders of the Rudolf Steiner Institute and the Washington Waldorf School.

Herbert Witzenmann was Leader of the Section for the Spiritual Striving of Youth, Goetheanum, Switzerland, and a philosopher, lecturer, and author.

Herbert Koepf (†2006), a teacher, farmer, and a researcher, was for nearly half a century one of the international leaders of the Biodynamic movement.

Virginia Sease is a member of the Executive Council of the worldwide Anthroposophical Society in Dornach, Switzerland, and is leader of the Section for Eurythmy, Speech, and Music.

RUDOLF STEINER INSTITUTE

Providing Summer Programs since 1974

Anthroposophical study and practice give us a larger spiritual context. In it we view the events and conditions of our time and develop means to participate in the creation of an equitable, harmonious, and sustainable world reality—one informed by soul and spirit.

- **Social, Cultural & Ecological Renewal**
- **Spiritual Inquiry**
- **Creativity & the Arts**
- **Education & Parenting**
- **Science & Spirit**
- **Programs for Children & Youth**

JOIN US THIS JULY 8-28, 2007 TO EXPLORE A VARIETY OF COURSES.

The Institute works to create an open community environment where individuals from diverse backgrounds will feel welcome to experience the spiritually-based knowledge of anthroposophy in the context of their own world view, beliefs and interests.

JOIN OUR MAILING LIST
www.steinerinstitute.org | 800-774-5191
registrar@steinerinstitute.org

Center
for
Anthroposophy

Waldorf Teacher Education & Renewal

Waldorf
High School
Teacher Education

Annual
Renewal Courses

Foundation Studies
in Anthroposophy
and the Arts

PO BOX 545, WILTON, NH 03086 PH: (603) 654-2566 FAX: (603) 654-5256
info@centerforanthroposophy.org   www.centerforanthroposophy.org

Do *you* want to change the world?

So do we...

...from the inside out

study groups

threefold social forms   LIBRARIES

service providers   sculpture

Camphill communities   research

CONFERENCES

seasonal festivals   astrosophy

youth programs

Biodynamic agriculture

therapists   Eurythmy   ECONOMICS

architecture

Waldorf education   medicine   meditation

speech &   drama   painting

consultants

PUBLISHING

In so many different ways,
members of the Anthroposophical Society in America are
actively participating in self and cultural transformation.

Get to know us better by visiting our
website at www.anthroposophy.org;
email us at information@anthroposophy.org;
or by calling our national office at 734-662-9355.

Anthroposophical Society in America
1923 Geddes Avenue, Ann Arbor, Michigan 48104
www.anthroposophy.org   Tel: 734.662.9355   Fax: 734.662.1727

CLASSIC" SELECTIONS FROM
THE *JOURNAL FOR ANTHROPOSOPHY*

Five very special issues composed of outstanding "classic" selections from the *Journal for Anthroposophy* are scheduled to be published. For each volume, a special editor will select and introduce a group of articles that have to do with a specific theme. The selections will be taken from issues dating as far back as the 1960's.

Existing or new subscribers will receive these "classic" editions as part of their regular subscriptions. Individual copies may be purchased as well. Current prices for either are available online at: http://www.anthroposophy.org/Orders/

These special editions are likely to become sought-after because of their unique content. Volume Number One, for example, has already been reprinted once. We will continue to make them widely available. SteinerBooks will offer them through their catalog and on-line.

Volume One – *Meeting Rudolf Steiner*, **Joan Almon, Editor.**

Firsthand accounts of living and working with Rudolf Steiner comprise this enticing edition. Steiner's personal qualities are brought to life through descriptions of a wide range of experiences – from intimate memories of his dinner table humor to vivid reports of his response to the burning of the first Goetheanum.

Volume Two – *Anthroposophy & Imagination*, **Kate Farrell, Editor.**

This collection reflects the view that true imagination, unlike mere fantasy, is a more-than-rational way of knowing; a natural bridge between matter and spirit; and a transformative state and stage of consciousness open to us all.

Volume Three – *Revisioning Society & Culture*, **Douglas Sloan, Editor**

The articles in this volume explore various anthroposophical perspectives of society and culture in the larger sense and help us to transform our dominant ways of knowing the world.

Volume Four – *Meeting Anthroposophy*, **Robert Hill, Editor**

The "meeting" with anthroposophy often connects with many threads in one's life and as one unravels them, a kind of personal mystery drama begins to unfold, a story that is at its base the mystery of ourselves, a story that has woven into it the karmic relationships that shape our lives and link us to our families, our friends and ultimately to the world. It is this mystery that draws us on and if we persist and adapt to this ever-changing interlocutor – anthroposophy – ever-new "meetings" await us, seemingly inexhaustible in number and content. These experiences may be characterized in such a way that can help us understand their mysterious power to reveal and transform. *To be published Autumn 2007*

Volume Five – *Science & Ecology*, **Arthur Zajonc, Editor**

Robert McDermott, Series Editor

Robert Mc Dermott, PhD, was president and is currently professor of philosophy and religion at the California Institute of Integral Studies. He was former professor and chair of the department of philosophy at Baruch College, CUNY.

Moving?

Please notify us six weeks before you move to ensure that you receive your next *Journal*.

Name _____

Old Address:

Address _____

City/State/Postal Code _____

New Address:

Address _____

City/State/Postal Code _____

Send to: *Journal For Anthroposophy*
               1923 Geddes Ave., Ann Arbor, MI 48104

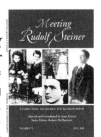